About the Authors

Binod C. Agrawal, currently, Director, TALEEM Research Foundation, Ahmedabad. Has his Ph.D. in Anthropology from University of Wisconsin. Was involved in the social evaluation of SITE and co-edited *Television and the Indian Child* (1987).

Kiran S. Karnik, currently Chief Operating Officer and Vice-President, Discovery channel in India. After graduation from Indian Institute of Management, Ahmedabad, joined technology management team Indian Space Research Organization, where he was Director, Development and Educational Communication Unit at Ahmedabad. He played a key role in the design, planning and implementation of SITE.

C. Lal, currently, Group Director in the area of Digital Communication in Space Applications Centre, ISRO, Ahmedabad. Holds his Master's degree in Electronics and Telecommunications from Allahabad University. He has been responsible for development of a number of satellite communication related technologies and led the team of engineers responsible for hardware development of SITE.

K. Vishwanath, Chief Producer, Development and Educational Communication Unit, ISRO, Ahmedabad had his Master's degree in Czechoslovakia in film production. Has produced several nationally acclaimed documentaries and educational films. He led the educational production team of science education during Satellite Instructional Television Experiment (SITE), 1975-76.

CHILDREN'S TELEVISION IN INDIA

A Situational Analysis

BINOD C. AGRAWAL
KIRAN S. KARNIK
C. LAL
K. VISHWANATH

CONCEPT PUBLISHING COMPANY, NEW DELHI - 110059

Views and opinions expressed in this report are those of its authors and do not necessarily represent or reflect the views of the respective Organization to whom they belong.

ISBN 81-7122-800-X

First Published 1999

Published and Printed by

Ashok Kumar Mittal
Concept Publishing Company
A/15-16, Commercial Block, Mohan Garden
NEW DELHI-110059 (India)

Phones : 5648039, 5649024
Fax : 091-11-5648053

ACKNOWLEDGEMENTS

IN THE preparation of this report several individuals assisted us. Dr. Mira Aghi acted as Consultant and provided inputs for the report based on her field work conducted in Delhi. We gratefully acknowledge her help in this regard. We take this opportunity to thank our colleagues Miss Anita Kamdar, Dr. Arbind Sinha, and Mr. Kalyan Raman who helped in the analysis and preparation of this report.

Ms. Omana Raghavan, Ms. S.K. Gujral and Mr. Gopal Krishnan Achari have been very patient in typing the whole manuscript and in completing it in time. To each of them we offer our sincere thanks. Thanks are also due to Mr. K.P. Nagar for collating the report.

CONTENTS

PART - I

RECOMMENDATIONS

* Need for a central, dedicated, well-equipped "mother facility": Centre for Children's TV or a Children's Laboratory.
* Other production facilities should be decentralized/dispersed to different linguistic/cultural regions.
* Involvement in programme production of large number of children and educational field agencies is essential.
* In particular, wide involvement of voluntary agencies and NGO's is desirable and suitable training should be provided to them for healthy competition.
* Children and educational field agencies and the involved voluntary groups/NGO's should be "networked" to the central "mother facility", which will provide guidance, assistance and training to them along with specialized facilities for programme production.
* Some video production equipment should be provided to selected field agencies.
* Team-mode of production-involving expert on children, content expert, communication researcher, producer and scriptwriter is recommended for quality and meaningful production.
* There is need to have a cadre of "dedicated" children's programmes producers and this must be given due recognition as a specialized field.
* Communication research being an essential component of the production needs special emphasis and required training.
* Researches related to television and children are few and fragmentary. Efforts should be made to encourage the area of research.
* Personnel working on children's programmes need specialized training. The planning and conduct of such specialized training courses needs attention and must be encouraged. For the present one-third of the training courses should be dedicated for children's television.

* Twenty per cent transmission time for children's programmes both for, and about children is recommended. Special attention needs to be given to "enrichment" programmes and to programmes that should be included in the general evening telecast.
* Special efforts are required to improve access of children to television sets—both in school, and in general community viewing situations.

INTRODUCTION

THE SITUATIONAL analysis report on Children's Television has been prepared at the request of UNICEF, New Delhi and Government of India. This report was commissioned by UNICEF to provide a blue-print for the medium-term work plan for UNICEF support to educational television for children in India. The initial terms of reference for the study were as follows:

(a) A thorough review of the existing situation of educational television for children in the country today. The analysis would, in detail, assess the national situation regarding production, research capacity, training potential, manpower, technical competence, strengths and weaknesses and overall growth potential. Both government and other existing production institutions would be reviewed.

(b) An analysis of the projected demand for educational programme production for INSAT and for primary school children and teachers in particular.

(c) After a review of (a) and (b) above, the report should detail the existing/projected gaps between supply and demand. In other words, what will need to be done regarding training, manpower increases, hardware requirements for production, facilities etc.

(d) Following the above, a systematic and comprehensive blue-print should be prepared for research-based production of educational programmes for children for various institutions, such as CIET, non-government, State departments of educational technology etc.

Given the fragmentary nature of information on the children's television in India, it became imperative to collate and synthesize the existing research on children's television. The methodology that has been followed for this study was guided by two considerations:

1. Given the state-of-art, first-hand interaction with all those involved in the children's television production, policy and research was considered essential. Also to locate and analyse documents and secondary data available within the television organizations—Doordarshan and other institutions involved in the production, training and research related to television in general and children's television in particular.
2. Television production demands a team of professionals and technologies. Keeping this in view, an interdisciplinary core team consisting of a producer, a media manager, and engineer and a communication researcher was formed. This four member team was further supported by two consultants—Dr. Mira B. Aghi, Child Psychologist and television formative researcher and Mr. B. K. Khurana, Director, Audience Research (TV). The core team took the responsibility of primary and secondary data collection in the respective areas of specialization—by visiting various institutions and organizations directly and indirectly involved in children's television programme production, research and planning. Formal and informal interviews with the concerned individuals supplemented by observations, provided the primary data. This was supplemented by additional data provided by the consultants. Detailed data on technology, future plans of television expansion, existing studio facilities, and television transmission was collected from various Doordarshan stations, Directorate of Doordarshan and the concerned organizations. Published reports and documents were also collected for reconstructing the historical analysis of children's television. The entire research conducted so far on children's television was reviewed, to draw major conclusions as an input for this report.

The report of the Working Group on Software for Doordarshan, entitled "*An Indian Personality for Television* (1985)", has discussed children's television in detail. Chapter XII on children's television is appropriately titled "Children: Victims or Beneficiaries?" to reflect the plight of children's television in the present circumstances. This Chapter provided a useful backdrop to this study. Another document which was of considerable help while preparing this report is: "*Television and the Indian Child: A Handbook* (1987)".

Data on the actual transmission, equipment availability, and production facilities, though collected from the original sources, vary when compared with data collected from other sources. It is because of several factors, including the different methods of estimation. Therefore, some of the statistics provided here may differ from the official figures. Efforts have been made to provide precise figures, but the same should be treated as an estimate at best.

The report is divided into five Chapters. In the first Chapter, an attempt has been made to provide an analytical perspective on Children's Television in India. It is followed by the content analysis of programme production, related to children's television in Chapter 2. In Chapter 3, Video Technology needed for children's television has been discussed. In Chapter 4, children's television related research has been synthesized to provide some guidelines for future production. In Chapter 5, training and management needed have been highlighted.

PART - II

1

CHILDREN'S TELEVISION IN INDIA
An Analytical Perspective

IN QUARTER century of the Indian Television, 'education' and children—as 40 per cent of the population—have been in the fore-front of discussion. The very inception of television in India is rooted in "social education". "Social education" in the early years of telecast was aimed at improving the "civic sense" of Delhi dwellers. The rationale for starting television was to provide education through a visual medium considered to be a successful means in other parts of the world. Credit for ushering television into the country partly goes to educationists who argued vehemently that the introduction of television would help improve the quality of education and increase the reach of education to those who could not be reached otherwise. Another persuasive argument for the introduction of television was that it would open up new means of cost-effective education outside the class room—both in 'non-formal' and 'distance-learning' situations.

In a recent article, an indepth review of Children's Television in India has been presented (Agrawal, in Press). In this review, it has been emphasized that the expansion of television followed a "wait and watch" philosophy. It was only introduced when experiences of other countries and experts had clearly shown the positive contributions that television can make in education and development. International agencies like the United Nations Educational, Scientific and Cultural Organization (UNESCO) also made a valuable contribution in supporting similar views, by financial support, and by bringing out a number of important publications on this subject. Also, several countries of the West, especially the United States of America (through Ford Foundation) took the initiative to promote the use of television for formal education. The Delhi School Television Project was a direct outcome of these efforts, and was started in 1961. Since then, there has been no going back, though the magnitude of the educational television in India cannot be called very satisfactory.

A few years after the introduction of the Delhi School Television Project, another stimulus for the use of television came from agricultural extension. To demonstrate the efficacy of television as a tool for development, a pilot project (Krishi-Darshan) was undertaken in the vital area of agriculture. This was inaugurated on 26 January, 1967. Thus, television enlarged its concern from education of children to instruction of farmers. Another major milestone in Indian television—and in children's television—was the Satellite Instructional Television Experiment (SITE). This experiment used the US ATS-6 satellite to transmit television programmes directly to about 2400 villages in different parts of the country. The broadcasts were received by community reception sets (one in each village), a majority of which were installed in schools. A substantial part of the transmission—1-1/2 hours out of 4 hours—was devoted to enrichment programmes for children in the age group of 5 to 12 years. An important new development in this context was the production of substantial proportion of these programmes by an agency other than Doordarshan (then a part of All India Radio) : The science education programmes were produced by ISRO.

The overall objectives of television from its inception have been broadly the same, as stated in a recent report : ". . . . to inform, educate as well as entertain with a view to creating awareness among the people about the nation's potentials for development and its problems, widening their horizon, and soliciting their participation in the implementation of the policies, plans and programmes of the Government for bringing about economic development and social change, achieving national security and promoting national integration" (Annual Report, 1983-84:1).

Recent Recommendations

In the context of Children's Television, it is worth noting the contents of two recent and important documents, viz., *An Indian Personality for Television* (1985) and the Annual Report 1983-84 of the Ministry of Information and Broadcasting. It may be a coincidence, but both reports came out at more or less the same time. Some discussion on these points would be worthwhile in the present context. It is no accident that a whole Chapter entitled "Children: Victims or Beneficiaries" (Chapter X) has been devoted in the "Report of the Working Group on Software Plan for Doordarshan" (*An Indian Personality for Television).* Also, a full chapter has to be devoted to 'Education' (Chapter VI: Educating the Masses : Resetting the Priorities). The main thrust in these two chapters can be summarized as follows:

1. Even after almost four decades, the nation has failed to utilize its vast educated manpower to eradicate illiteracy. Therefore, highest priority should be given to use of television for education and literacy based on the experience gained from several television pilot projects conducted in the country. At the same time, "the debate on the educational uses of television should not be allowed to cloud the basic priorities of Indian Educational Planning" (*An Indian Personality for Television*—Part II, Chapter VI).
2. Most of the children's programmes of Doordarshan seem to have been designed for the 'upper class' urban children. The television programmes meant for children "should be directed primarily towards disadvantaged children in rural and urban areas". (*An Indian Personality for Television,* Part II, Chapter X.)
3. At least 15 to 20 per cent of the total transmission time should be allocated for children's programmes and there should be a separate section within Doordarshan stations devoted exclusively to programming for children.

In the other report, Doordarshan has crystallised its main objectives in the following words:

(a) to act as a catalyst for social change,
(b) to promote national integration,
(c) to stimulate a scientific temper in the minds of the people,
(d) to disseminate the message of family planning as a means of control and family welfare,
(e) to provide essential information and knowledge in order to stimulate greater agricultural production,
(f) to promote and help preserve environmental and ecological balance,
(g) to highlight the need for social welfare measures including welfare of women, children and the less privileged,
(h) to promote interest in games and sports, and
(i) to create values of appraisal of artistic and cultural heritage *(Annual Report 1983-84:25).*

It is obvious that there is a gap between what is expected from the medium and what Doordarshan plans to do for 'education' (which is not mentioned) and 'children', who are mentioned only in passing. Any attempt to correct the situation would require policy intervention at the national level, which must be tried. Also, it is possible that Doordarshan has completely left out the area of "education" from their active production purview as it is now being taken care of by the concerned ministries and departments of the Government of India.

Ministry of Human Resources Development (earlier Ministry of Education and Culture) issued National Guidelines for Educational Broadcasting (NGEB) in 1983. The guidelines define the "Role of Educational Broadcasting both for radio and television." It is among other things expected to act "as a major component of the non-formal education system—providing an alternative approach to the education of out of school children, youth and adults" (NGEB, 1983:1). Further, universalization of elementary education for girls, rural and urban poor have been considered as areas of priority. Though there is a national debate in full swing on the "new educational policy" there has been a policy statement which states that "Educational Broadcasting should be integrated within the total educational system" and "the responsibility for policy and management of educational broadcasting should be with the educational authority" (NGEB 1983:2). Recognizing the linguistic and cultural heterogenity, the guidelines recommend taking "cognizance of localized needs, differences in language and culture and other similar phenomena be so organized that it can be regionalized and localized" (NGEB 1983:2). A comparison of the stated objectives for the use of television for children may not be at variance but certainly differs in emphasis between the 'user' and 'service' ministry. It is well reflected in the way Doordarshan treats educational and children-related programme production, transmission and even the categorization of the educational and children-related programmes.

Telecast of Children's Television

For the convenience of classification and analysis presentation, the total telecast in relation to education and children falling in the age group of 0-14 is classified in Table 1.1.

The term "Enrichment School Telecast" includes all those telecasts that are meant for school children from 5 to 11 years of age and expected to be viewed in school on a community television. It is targeted at children of two specific age groups: 5 to 8 years, and 9 to 11 years. Enrichment School Telecasts include those programmes which have educational content with specific learning objectives but not directly linked with any specific syllabus, a programming technique that was followed for a large

TABLE 1.1: **Broad Distribution and Classification of Children Television**

Sr. No.	*Type of Television Programme*	*Enrichment School Telecast*	*Exclusive School Telecast*	*Evening General Telecast*
1.	For children	INSAT Areas	Few Metropolitan	All Stations
2.	About children	For Teachers in INSAT Areas	—	Spots by UNICEF Bombay "Palavi"

majority of SITE children's programmes. In this category, a few programmes are also being telecast for school teachers to improve their teaching ability and knowledge, but these programmes can qualify to be called "about children". The enrichment programmes are received in all areas covered under satellite direct telecast by INSAT and are also rebroadcast by a number of TV transmitters. On school days, 45 minutes of programmes are transmitted each morning in Hindi, Oriya, Telugu, Marathi and Gujarati for direct reception as well as for rebroadcast by transmitters in the concerned States, including the transmitters at Ranchi, Gorakhpur, Cuttack, Hyderabad, Nagpur and Rajkot. For each of these regions, it works out to be about 8 per cent of the total scheduled telecast time. At present, the production responsibility is shared between Doordarshan and the Central Institute of Educational Technology (CIET). In Doordarshan, the major responsibility of these programmes lies with Upgrah Doordarshan Kendras at Delhi, Cuttack and other INSAT stations along with CIET. Studios are also being set up specially for production of educational programmes in six States, and this is being done by the concerned State Institute of Educational Technology (SIET). After the SIET studios become operational, the total production responsibility for this category of programmes would rest with CIET and the SIETs.

The term "Exclusive School Telecast" includes those programmes which are transmitted for class room instruction. At present, stations like Bombay, Delhi and Madras transmit programmes for this kind of viewing. They are telecast in the morning hours and repeated in the afternoon, but the total transmission time devoted for this purpose is small. It varies from zero (as several stations do not transmit programmes for schools) to about 5 per cent (in Delhi). It is important to mention that "Exclusive School Telecast" tends to be higher secondary school children. All these programmes by and large relate to some syllabus and production based directly on text book lessons. There are no "exclusive telecast" about children either for parents or for teachers. At present, all these programmes are being produced by Doordarshan as a part of their regular production.

"Evening General Telecast" contains all those programmes which are broadcast along with programmes for adults. These programmes are meant for all age groups of children. For example, it ranges from "Disney Cartoons" to Films Division documentaries on children. Agencies like UNICEF provide spots "about children" on "health and nutrition" directed at adults. An estimate of such "Evening General Telecast" is provided in Table 1.2, based on the programme content analysis of what Doordarshan refers to as "Area Specific Programmes." Table 1.2 shows a great variation from 0.12 per cent (in Hyderabad) to Cuttack, where it is 7.06 per cent. All these programmes are either produced or procured by Doordarshan. The most important point to be noted here is the overwhelming and over-shadowing preponderance of general adult telecast for individual home viewing in the company of elder relatives by the children. In the community television viewing situation, the utilization by children is minimal in all three categories due to limited access to television. Table 1.3 shows that in six INSAT coverage areas, there are 1653 school television sets for an estimated children population of 1,70,41,000. The picture is not very different even in the metropolitan cities like Delhi.

TABLE 1.2: **Percentage Distribution of General Evening Telecast for Children**

Sr. No.	Name of the Station	*Children*	*Adults*
1.	Ranchi	0.97	99.03
2.	Delhi Channel - I	3.19	96.81
3.	Delhi Channel - II	2.56	97.44
4.	Jallandhar	2.44	97.56
5.	Nagpur	2.90	97.10
6.	Madras	1.87	98.13
7.	Bombay	6.72	93.28
8.	Calcutta	5.99	94.01
9.	Cuttack	7.06	92.74
10	Hyderabad	0.12	97.88
11.	Delhi*	1.60	98.40
12.	Gulbarga	1.19	98.81
13.	Gorakhpur	5.48	97.52
	Average	2.49	97.51

Source : Audience Research Unit, New Delhi.

Note : The data for the month of September 1985 has been computed. Due to lack of data, analyses of all stations are not mentioned here.

* Upgrah Doordarshan Station. This station produces programmes for three centres namely Jaipur, Muzaffarpur and Raipur.

TABLE 1.3: **Distribution of Community Televisions for Exclusive School Viewing Station in INSAT covered Areas**

Sr. No.	*Name of the Television Station*	*Number of Television Schools*	*Expected Number of Children to view Television*
1.	Cuttack	614	2129,200
2.	Gorakhpur	26	4367,200
3.	Hyderabad	540	2576,600
4.	Nagpur	276	2593,200
5.	Rajkot	197	2234,800
6.	Ranchi	0	3140,000
	Total	1653	17041,000

Source : Audience Research Unit, Doordarshan, New Delhi

Note :

1. Data are provided for the month of August, 1985.
2. Figures show estimated 40 per cent of the targeted children in the total population.
3. Telecast is 8.0 per cent of the local transmission.

Another important issue to be taken into consideration is the language of these programmes. A majority of them are being telecast in Hindi or English. While Hindi provides a larger coverage of clientele, English provides a microscopic coverage for elite children for television viewing. The significant conclusion that can be drawn from the analysis is that only a fraction of the total children population have access to view television of their relevance. In the small percentage of children's programmes, a very minor proportion is for children of 'pre-school' age (below 5 years of age). In fact, there are hardly any programmes at all for them. In sum, as compared to their needs or their population, there is a very little television telecast for children. Further, whatever is being telecast cannot be viewed due to limited access. What is viewed, leaves much to be desired in terms of both quality and relevance of the programmes.

Given the limitation of telecast time and access, it is essential to work out the details of transmission time. At the same time, it would be even more urgent to work out the details of production philosophy and plan of educational television for children.

VIDEO USE BY CHILDREN

Very little quantitative information is available anywhere in the country to indicate the extent of use of video by children either in the schools or in the home-viewing situation. Observations have indicated that children, especially pre-school children in video-owning homes, do have access to a few pre-recorded English video cassettes containing cartoons, some songs and some of the pre-school programmes of foreign origin. These cassettes are being viewed by the pre-school children as and when parents want them to see or they could persuade their parents to show them. Older children in "video homes" too have some access to cartoons and to very few children's programmes. However, 'commercial' films both Indian and foreign (basically from the West) are seen in considerable quantity by children of all ages in "video homes" and often (through hired equipment) by children in "non video homes" also.

Some of the more prosperous schools have already acquired video cassette recorders and do occasionally show 'educational' programmes. However, these being beyond the purview of this report, no quantitative data was collected on the use of video either in homes or in schools.

PRODUCTION TECHNOLOGY FOR CHILDREN'S TELEVISION

The technological advance in recent years has been so great that systems unthinkable a few years back are a reality today. Its impact is being felt in every domain of human endeavour. Video technology is no exception. These advances have facilitated the incorporation of more number of functions, reliable operation, ruggedization, precision, automation and ease of operation. The rapid strides in the use of Very Large Scale Integrated (VLSI) technology, use of digital techniques coupled with the new developments in the field of microprocessors have made all this possible. While this is a technological scene at the international level, within the country Doordarshan too has made major changes in its equipment and its studios. The biggest change has been the switch-over to colour, rendering obsolete the old monochrome equipment. New generation portable and lightweight electronic field production and news gathering (EFP/ENG) equipment has substantially replaced the film cameras used for outdoor recording. In the process, though the earlier equipment has become obsolete, it continues to be listed as "available equipment," without any effective use. For example, film processing equipment available at some of the Doordarshan stations now have very little use. Similarly, old one inch video tape recorders, which are not colour compatible and the old two inch VTR's are just lying in the studios. While there is a major effort to introduce new equipment (especially colour equipment) to completely replace old and monochrome equipment, analysis indicates that Doordarshan staff is forced to use monochrome equipment in order to replay old programmes. Sometimes, the lack of sufficient colour equipment also necessitates the use of monochrome equipment to produce programmes (see Table 1.4). This factor especially affects the production of children's television programmes, as they generally get very low priority. Another technology problem relates to the lack of full component of equipment in many of the Doordarshan studios and special effects equipments required for children's television programme production. Augmentation and replacement of old equipment and identification and procurement of special equipment for children's programme would be essential for improving the technical quality of children's television. This would have to include equipment for special effects, animation and post-production facilities.

TABLE 1.4: **Distribution of Colour and Black & White Programme Production by Selected Stations**

Sr. No.	*Name of the Station*	*Colour*	*Black & White*
1.	Ranchi	91.00	9.00
2.	Delhi Channel - I	97.80	2.20
3.	Delhi Channel - II	99.20	0.80
4.	Jallandhar	85.00	15.00
5.	Nagpur	88.00	12.00
6.	Madras	35.20	64.80
7.	Bombay	95.70	4.30
8.	Calcutta	83.00	17.00
9.	Cuttack	1.00	99.00
10	Hyderabad	60.00	40.00
11.	Gulbarga	73.00	27.00
12.	Delhi	72.00	28.00
13.	Gorakhpur	73.53	3.00
	Average	73.53	26.47

Source : Audience Research Unit, Doordarshan, New Delhi.

Note : Data are provided for the month of Septemebr, 1985.

CHILDREN'S TELEVISION PROGRAMME PRODUCTION

Earlier, all children's programmes were produced by Doordarshan. The only major exception was made during SITE, when some 180 science education programmes were produced by the Indian Space Research Organization. With the start of the INSAT System, the responsibility for production of educational programmes has been taken up by the Department of Education. The Central Institute of Educational Techno- logy (CIET), New Delhi, and State Institutes of Educational Technology (SIET) located in the six "INSAT States" have taken on the task of producing educational programmes for children. These programmes are supplied in the form of 45 minutes capsules for each State/language to Doordarshan for transmission in the morning (from 9 am to 12.45 pm). While CIET is making considerable efforts to produce programmes, the SIETs would take some time to become fully operational. The requirements of "enrichment school telecasts" are therefore met with the help of production by some of the Doordarshan stations also, especially by the Upgrah Doordarshan Kendras. Other television stations are also producing children's programmes which are being telecast as a part of the "exclusive for School" and "evening general" telecast. A few foreign programmes from English speaking countries and Eastern European countries are also being telecast. There is also some amount of repetition of programmes. A serial meant for pre-school children is being telecast on Sunday mornings. On the whole, television production "for children" and "about children" is falling short, both in quantity and quality. There is need to improve both these aspects.

Analysis from various Doordarshan stations, CIET, SIET and other agencies involved in the production of children's television shows that since SITE days, when studio and other facilities were considered a serious constraint for production, the position seems to have improved. It is very comforting to hear today that adequate facilities and funds are available for production of children's programme, and are not posing any serious problem for CIET, and the same will be true for SIETs, when they become operational. Though major additions to production facilities has taken place in Doordarshan, these facilities are only minimally used for children's television programmes.

Based on the various information available and observations, children's television programme production of all types mentioned earlier can be characterized as production of compromises done by producers who act merely as facilitators, and dependent upon script writers or others who act as programme designer. The quality of the programme greatly depends upon individual producer's creativity and initiative. Production plans remain a responsibility of the producer. There is a lack of equipment facilities. Producers do not know about the actual utilization of the programmes. Research inputs are lacking. Even where there are researchers, they are not up-to-date in their knowledge or do not provide appropriate inputs. Producers are lacking any data based guidelines to know how learning takes place among children and what kind of formats facilitate learning, say a drama format as compared to a lecture or demonstration format.

While CIET is reasonably comfortable in terms of equipment, Doordarshan stations outside Delhi are not only short of equipment, but production of children's television programmes gets very low priority. For example, for the production of four children programmes in a metropolitan television station, the Producer gets one half shift of studio time. Each programme is expected to be of about 20 minutes duration. Only film equipment will be made available for shooting in the school laboratories. Even in the Upgrah Doordarshan Kendras, a similar situation exists. In these conditions, Producers tend to cut corners, making programme formats as simple as possible.

Production Management

A common expression heard was "come hell or high water, the scheduled programme has to go on air" which implies that production and dubbing has to be finished within the chunk of time allotted. If the time allotted is adequate, one would have no reason to complain; but it was found, as mentioned earlier, that each Producer has to produce an average of four programmes per month leading to poor quality of production. This inevitably leads to compromises in production. While it is important that scheduled programmes go on air on time, an excessively tight schedule creates tension, frustrations, results in production of poor quality programmes and develops an attitude of indifference.

At present, the needs for transmission are so high that producers at times use clippings from 15 to 20 years old films produced by various organizations and insert them in the so-called new programmes. What can one really expect if a 20-minute programme has clippings from films produced in the 1960s?

This situation could be made easier at this stage if a method is evolved by which a large amount of candid shots are stored for such programme production. Appropriate methods for storage and retrieval should therefore be evolved for this purpose.

Other aspects that need attention include transport, reference room, video archives, library (film, video, still photographs and books), rehearsal room, property room, puppet libraries and animation units, all of which would help in both increasing efficiency and producing better programmes.

Professional and efficient management of the production facilities and the production process is another essential aspect. This will ensure that the creative team gets the maximum possible support and that the limited facilities are optimally used. Organizational structure, management methods and operating procedures are also crucial elements of the system.

Not all Producers in Doordarshan, CIET, SIET and other production agencies are appropriately trained for general television production. Even those who are, understandably feel that producing for children requires some additional inputs in terms of understanding the child's needs and thought processes. Special training for this is necessary, despite the fact that many of the Producers may have been originally trained in education or have teaching experience. For this, they would like to undergo a short, comprehensive training programme, which would highlight the child's development process. The need was felt, particularly with reference to rural and urban deprived children. The specialized training, they feel, would help them in conveying ideas in a manner that is understood by the children. It would also add to their insight and help them in discussing the scripts with writers and subject-matter specialists. At present, they find this difficult, due to lack of adequate information and knowledge about their "target audiences." In the case of the INSAT-relayed enrichment telecasts, very few Producers had ever visited the target area, though they all felt that such visits would help them in producing meaningful programmes. Similar observations have been made by the Working Group for Software Plan for Doordarshan (*An Indian Personality for Doordarshan,* 1985).

Towards Team Mode of Production

Given the complexity of the subject-matter of children's programmes and the limited experiences of the Producers, it is strongly felt that the production process should be a team effort (which is elaborated in later chapters). Inputs of different kinds are required, and these necessitate the working together of experts from different disciplines. While the producer is the leader of the team, unless he/she is able to obtain efficient help from the other team members, the entire effort becomes futile. This requires good inter-personal skills, and the ability to be an organizer and a resource manager, who can facilitate group work and get the best out of the various team members. At the same time, the Producer should not be at the mercy of the other team members, and must assert himself.

Commitment is required on everyone's part, so that each member of the team pulls his weight and shares the production responsibility at various stages of production.

Specialized training for each of the production staff was also an immediate need felt by the Producers. With the time factor playing such a crucial role, most of the Producers mentioned that if every crew member was a specialist in his/her area (be it a lighting assistant or a floor manager), it would help in communicating one's requirements and instructions better, and in getting the job done faster and much more efficiently.

A point was made to the effect that working relationships and work ethos needs to be extended to other professionals like script writers and content specialists working in the team. Producers should have access and be able to talk and discuss details with other professionals.

At one place it was gathered that the Producer receives a readymade script, which he has to shoot within a week. It is almost as if it were a silent order. If the Producer has any questions or doubts regarding the content or script, he hardly has any time to seek clarifications or clear doubts. From experience, one can say that is extremely important for a Producer to sit with the content expert, script writer and communication researcher to discuss and clarify every detail of what he is going to produce. The quality of programme is bound to suffer in the absence of such working conditions.

Experiences so far

Given the limited television telecast for the age group 0-14 years within and outside the school, there are very few studies related to children and television in India. Agrawal and Aghi (in Press) have brought out an annotated Bibliography on the available research on children's television. These researches can be classified into three categories. These are:

1. Formative research related to children's television.
2. Press Research.
3. Summative Research.

Formative Research

The span of formative research covers a period of about 25 years, beginning from 1961 when Delhi School Television Project was initiated. Neurath (nd) has reported about the "careful analysis" of the needs of Delhi students before the television production started. These programmes were meant for higher secondary school students in the age group of 13 to 16 years, studying in classes IX, X and XI. However, there is no detailed document to indicate if efforts were made to draw the Delhi students profile or about the methods followed by the researches to assess the students' educational needs. From all accounts available, a series of serious discussions were held among the educationists, programme producers and experts (both national and international) before launching the project (Kumar and Jai Chandiram, 1967). The School Television Project decided "to put out a programme of direct, systematic, organized in-school televised instruction" (Sehgal, 1979:82).

In 1975 also, 'enrichment' programmes for primary school children were produced and telecast in Delhi for the institutions run by the Delhi Municipal Corporation, no such research efforts were made. (*Television in India 1985:5*).

In SITE, major efforts were mounted for formative research for children's television programme production [Aghi 1977, Aghi (in Press) and Trivedi (in Press)]. Similar efforts were followed in post-SITE phase, in the SITE Continuity areas (Agarwal and Choudhary 1984a and 1984b).

Formative researches essentially helped in defining the "target group", their entry skill, socio-cultural and educational 'profiles', and informational needs. In some cases, researches also throw light on the impediments, both psychological and socio-economic, in appropriate utilization of television messages. For example, Behari and Gupta (1979) indicated, among other things, that Rajasthan rural children were not sent to school as majority of them were required at home to do petty labour. Also, early marriage, late admission and poverty lead to high drop-out and absenteeism from the school. Singh and Singh (1984), while evaluating the educational needs of Orissa rural school children, found they wish to view television programmes covering health and hygiene, general knowledge and moral education.

What has emerged from these studies is the revalidation of some of the earlier hunches and beliefs of the educationists and communicators. In a very general and broad way, some of these findings, though very area-specific and tentative in nature about rural children between 5 to 12 years of age of both sexes are given below:

1. Children constitute a larger proportion of television viewers than adult males or females. They are also the most avid television viewers.

2. Pre-production or formative researches are crucial for tailoring television programmes to the needs and requirements of the children.
3. Systematic research-based programme production can ensure quality production and will achieve desired effects on children.
4. Very little formative researches have been conducted relating to urban children, though some efforts have been made for rural children.
5. Emphasis has to be laid on "team mode or production" of children's television programme. The team—consisting of producer, script writer, content expert, researcher and "production staff"—must be formed for producing meaningful children's television programmes.
6. Regardless of language or region, use of simple and spoken language help better comprehension of the programmes. In most formative researches, improvement (simplification) in the programme language has been recommended.
7. Programme pre-tests have shown that the information/content load should be in accordance with the mental level of the children, and educational objectives of the television programmes should be properly specified. These have been generally lacking in the past.
8. There is no clear indication whether there is special preference for 'child' or 'adult' characters in children's television programmes. The formative research studies have provided varying conclusions in this issue.
9. Separate television programmes should be produced for children of different age groups.
10. There is high appeal and comprehension of visual presentation rather than verbal dialogue. Visual presentations also hold the attention and interest level of the children.

Process Research

Most of the process research or feedback studies have been in the form of small, individual-programme studies, providing micro-level programme—specific results as an input for programme production. The most important conclusion that can be drawn from feedback studies is that programme feedback is an important means of getting inputs for future programme production and also a means by which mid-course corrections can be made in those programmes which are presented as 'serials'. Trivedi (1977), while conducting a feedback study of a Gujarati children's programme, indicated that the programme successfully held the attention and interest level of the children. It was observed that familiarity with the story characters was an added and important factor in holding their attention.

The most comprehensive feedback study on children's TV viewing was conducted during SITE on a continuous basis, for the academic year 1975-1976. (See Bhaskaran, P. assisted by I. Patel 1977). On every children's transmission day, data was collected from the children of Classes I to V from 24 schools spread over six States. It was observed that programmes meant for the students of Class I to V were also viewed by other children and children from higher classes. The comprehension of the programmes was 40 per cent for the students of classes I to III, and 58 to 90 per cent among the students of Class IV and V. In general, non-educational programmes were comprehended best and students—irrespective of comprehension level—liked such programmes. These studies have shown the importance and utility of feedback for improving the quality of television programmes.

Summative Research

Except very few comprehensive 'effect' studies—notable among them being those of Neurath (nd), Shukla and Kumar (1977), Rahman (1977) and Aghi (1977)—there are not many studies to measure the effects of educational television on children. The results of these evaluations have shown that viewing of television programmes stimulated interest and seemed to facilitate the formation of a 'scientific' attitude. By and large, television viewing children have done better in the tests than non-television-viewing children. Results have shown gains in language development and interest in acquiring knowledge as a result of television viewing among the children of Class III and V. Interaction between the teachers and students increased as a result of television viewing. Television viewing improved children's desire to ask, know and learn. These studies have shown positive and desired effects of television on children, which can be further improved by way of producing need-based, quality television programmes.

Television Utilization by Children

Television utilization by children seems to be very limited in the schools.

No data is available from the individual households about the degree of television utilization. (The term 'utilization' here means the actual viewing of television by children, especially the educational programmes and programmes about children). Bhaskaran (1977) found that due to a number of operational problems—like power failure, current fluctuations, and audio video technical problems—on a number of occasions children could not see television meant for them during SITE in a community viewing situation. Phutela (1984), while studying Delhi School, suggested that for appropriate utilization of children's television programmes there is need for improvement in the school organization and management, competencies of various school functionaries, and training of teachers in the use of the programmes. Goel (1984) and several others have indicated under-utilization of television due to non-repair of television sets and several other factors that should be corrected.

Production Research Needs

Except Upgrah Doordarshan Kendra, New Delhi, Calcutta and Hyderabad, there has been little effort to provide research input in children's television programme production in Doordarshan. Fortunately, CIET does have research staff for this purpose. But it is difficult to provide actual research-production interaction and inputs of research in production. In Ahmedabad, research inputs are available for the Kheda Communications Project. But then this station has produced few programmes for children except syllabus school telecast, transmitted along with general evening telecast. Apart from the frustrations reflected by the researchers, efforts were also made to evaluate the Producers needs for research inputs. The generalized picture that emerged is provided here.

Inadequate research inputs was one aspect mentioned by almost every Producer. Some did not clearly spell it out as research, but each one frankly felt that they had absolutely no knowledge about their potential viewers except for their age. Continuous and regular research is lacking almost everywhere. Producers sincerely felt that information and knowledge about their target audiences would help them in presenting concepts in a manner that is familiar and not alien to the children's environmental surrounding. Not only did they express a need to somehow increase interaction between researchers and Producers, but also felt that Producers must be compulsorily asked to go to the areas they are producing for, and even play the role of an objective observer during the pretesting exercises.

Much of this, of course, is feasible only if the production agency has a fairly equal proportion of Producers and researchers. In one of the places visited, there was a single researcher for all Producers. However dedicated the researcher may be, it would be simply impossible for him to do an efficient job. In such places, the script writer or the content expert plays the dual role of a researcher-cum-script writer. The research input here only consists of the reading that may have been done before actually writing the script. This obviously is only one part of the research input. One can think of several other inputs from research like script testing, pre-testing of programmes, etc. Feedback on the programmes is also quite rare. Programmes once shot get completely forgotten. The Producers have absolutely no idea as to whether their programmes were seen by the children, how many saw it or what kind of impact it had. Many Producers felt that this factor affects their motivation to produce better programmes. They felt that unless a systematic interaction pattern with the researchers was evolved it would remain a shot in the dark.

2

PROGRAMME PRODUCTION

THE BROAD distribution of children's programmes telecast by Doordarshan was described and analysed in the previous Chapter. The analysis focused on the classification and quantity of programmes telecast for children. It would be desirable to further analyse the process and production techniques followed so far in India. Some of the programme production techniques as indicated in Chapter 1 remained at an experimental level, whereas others have become a part of the regular production methods. In this Chapter, the work being done in three agencies involved in children's television production has been examined. The three agencies are Doordarshan, Central Institute of Educational Technology (NCERT), and Development and Educational Communication Unit (ISRO).

What do we know about Children?

It sounds naive to think that we know all about children without researching about them, without ever asking what they would like to see on television or what are their preferences about television programmes. So far, children in Indian television have been ignored, talked-down-to or been mere 'extras' in programmes for adults. It seems that children react by often rejecting the television programmes, by not watching the programmes ostensibly for them. The vulnerability of this medium has been little understood by television producers and policy-makers because almost no efforts have been made to investigate whether (i) the television is on when children's programmes are being telecast; and (ii) is television being turned off by the children during this period. From several accounts and studies a very small percentage of children actually watch children's programmes that are meant for them.

Another view expressed is that the children's television is not informative, inspiring and interesting, hence they do not watch it. Viewers, producers and educationists have many unpleasant things to say about children's television. A very serious question has been raised: "Why are children's programmes so childish and silly" on Doordarshan. One of the major reasons is that children get the lowest priority in several areas in terms of quality of producers for children's television programme production, facilities provided for such production and time allocation for transmission. Keeping these factors as given, the attempt here is to document the present state of children's programme production.

Production of Enrichment School Programmes

There is a more than a decade-old tradition producing enrichment programmes for school children in the age group of 5 to 12 years of age, as indicated in Chapter 1. It started during SITE, when 90 minutes of educational television programmes were broadcast daily to enrich the child's learning experience at school. The need to move to enrichment type programmes was dictated by the varying syllabus and school schedules in the vast areas to be covered by SITE. As early as 1971 according to the Working Group on Educational Technology report (1978) television was among several mass media to support the teaching-learning process. However, the debate on the use of television, whether for enrichment or syllabus-based education continues, and there are both pragmatic and pedagogic differences on this issue. Agrawal (in Press) indicates these differences in the following words,

> ".......in a multi-cultural and multi-linguistic country like India telecasting of syllabus based programmes at any given time would be useful to a small minority. In order to have high multiplier effects, it was felt desirable to produce enrichment programmes. The opposite argument is that enrichment programmes would not be useful to any specific target group."

The production of enrichment television programmes broadly follows the SITE guidelines for production in the Upgrah Doordarshan Kendras located at Delhi (for Jaipur, Muzaffarpur and Raipur), Hyderabad (for Hyderabad and Gulbarga), Cuttack (for Sambalpur), Ranchi, Gorakhpur, Nagpur and Rajkot. In a few cities like Madras, a similar approach is followed for primary school telecast. Most of the children's television producers are inducted into production after a degree in education. While there is a difference between the approach followed by Doordarshan and

CIET due to equipment availability and other resources, Doordarshan produces programmes on the basis of topics suggested by CIET.

Observations indicate that the team mode of production is not followed in all Doordarshan stations. In fact, this notion was considered almost foreign by one of the Station Directors. In places like Hyderabad, there is some interaction between the researcher, producer and script writer. However, even thereafter the subjects/themes/ideas are worked out by the production team, they are handed over to subject experts or teachers to prepare scripts, rehearse talent and collect all necessary materials required for the programme. Due to the high load of production (3 programmes a week), the producer is forced to leave all the responsibilities to the script writer in terms of content, format and other details of the programme. Generally, the producer acts only as a programme "coordinator" of various persons and activities, which include teachers, script writers, studio facilities, studio time and artistes. Finally the producers's job is merely "editing shots".

As of now, it is observed that very few producers have had the opportunity to visit the target areas for which they produce programmes. Seldom do they talk to the children who are their target group. Also, they have very little idea about how their programmes are being received and what children think about them. Researchers have made attempts to provide children's need assessments and audience profiles. But these are not put to any use because of lack of encouragement and guidance given to producers. A few producers do feel the need for a team mode of production, and would want script writers and educationists to work on the team to produce meaningful programmes.

Exclusive School Production

Production of "exclusive school" television for upper primary and secondary schools is amongst the oldest areas of television production in India, and began in 1961. The initial method of production followed a typical "class room/teacher-lecture" approach. Laboratory experiments were demonstrated in a "class room" by the teacher. At present, in three cities namely, Bombay, Delhi and Madras, television programmes for "exclusively school" purpose are produced. A large number of such programmes were also produced by DECU/ISRO and transmitted by Pij; however, these were broadcast in the evening "general telecast" slot.

The guidelines for the production of these syllabus-based programmes are worked out in cooperation and consultation with the State educational authorities. For example, in case of Delhi, Delhi Directorate of Education works in close cooperation with Delhi Doordarshan. In Bombay, at present, all the exclusive school television broadcast are in the morning and repeated in the afternoon. Bombay Doordarshan follows a schedule under which English lessons are telecast on Monday for Class V and Wednesday for Class VI. For Class VIII, science lessons are telecast on Friday. In Madras, the programme telecast schedule is worked out in consultation with the State Educational Technology Cell. Programmes are produced for several classes of secondary school like VIII and X. These programmes are syllabus based. In Delhi, the programme production for higher secondary and other classes is being done by Delhi Doordarshan. These programmes are meant for urban, school-going children. In most cases, these programmes are being produced by one-time school-teachers, who serve as producers or as presenters; the assumption being that they would be able to take care of educational and content aspects of the programme. In another Doordarshan station, while scripts are written by school teachers, they are vetted and presented by a college teacher, with the aim of assuring and overseeing the educational content of the programme. The producer has the primary responsibility of production as in the case of enrichment school programmes. All the problem areas indicated earlier apply in the case of such programmes too.

The Evening General Telecast for Children

This category includes children's programme which contain elements of information and education or 'entertainment' and are broadcast as part of the evening "general telecast". These three words, 'entertainment', 'information' and 'education' have been so much over-used that one wonders if the producers do not need resensitisation to the concepts and their meaning. The word 'entertainment' is used for all those programmes in which there is no direct instruction involved. However, the producers do not seem greatly concerned about whether the children see the programme or not or even whether they get pleasure from viewing it. The bulk of the programmes are produced as a result of the initiative of the assigned children's programme producers—who invariably define for themselves what entertainment is, what information is or even what values are to be encouraged and catered to. In this category, there are a large number of programmes including those produced by outside agencies like Films Division or programmes produced in other countries, as indicated in Chapter 1. As most of the programmes are produced on individual initiatives, there is considerable scope for "creative expression", which may or may not be of children's liking. Several formats have been used in such productions. Duration of the programmes also vary. Two examples will provide some insights into these issues.

The producer in charge at Bangalore, with stage experience, concentrates on magazine formats—three to four items which would include a skit, music and an education bit thrown in, which could range from topical items of the day to science education. There is an innate awareness of the needs of the children on the part of the producer, who ensures that children from schools participate in many programmes. The show goes on air between 7 and 7.30 p.m. fortnightly, thanks to the pressure of other necessary local and national programming. The targeted age group is 4 to 14 years. The producer picks and chooses ideas/items offered by the schools and children's organisations, besides her own ideas and that of her peers. Since there is a constant flow of offerings of various items by children's groups and schools, the range of selection is wide. For quality purposes, 'offered' items are auditioned before recording, either at their work places or in the studio. Since participation of children is an important part of the programmes, there is an equally tremendous audience response, both on the part of parents and children.

At Madras, the transmission of children's programmes takes a different shape:

On Wednesday	=	15 minutes for below 8 years.
On Saturday	=	30 minutes for age group up to 14 years
		Both programmes are in Tamil, and one monthly programme on Sunday morning for 30 minutes is in English.

For generation of the programme idea, the paths are the same: scripts through letters, offered items by schools or dance-cum-music schools, or ideas/topics suggested to these groups. The format adopted here is slightly different from other centres—that is to say, there is a definite purpose to each of the items in the children's magazine. A typical programme may contain:

- — a dance or music on national integration
- — one spoken word item—drama/interview on nutrition or on moral values
- — an information item e.g., visit to a place

The producer prefers to knit these items together by using a child compere. The reason for this, the producer says, is that children would like to emulate their counterparts.

Producers necessarily tend to depend a great deal on their background—theatre, literature, education—and to use this as their strong point in their programme production. One of the producers, with an academic background in theatre became so abstruse in his productions (from the point of his peers, one supposes) that he was persuaded to shift to other assignments.

But, in talking with him or with other producers, it became apparent that their creative presentation or production techniques were based either on their own thumb rules, audience responses or sheer instinct. The subjective instinct leads to various conclusions. For example, one producer felt strongly that children do not like other children appearing in programmes, as it produces an inferiority complex; and that a child compere boosts confidence and identification in children.

The procedure followed for the selection of programme ideas, formats and presentation techniques is almost identical at other Doordarshan Kendras, though one may observe minor variations. Another common characteristic of these programmes is that a majority of them are produced 'live' i.e., during the transmission itself. One estimate shows that 80 to 90 per cent of such programmes are 'live' and invariably a play (drama) format is utilized, due to equipment constraints.

The producers responsible for the production of these programmes come from diverse backgrounds and lack the appropriate educational background to produce children's programme on a large number of educational topics.

Programme Production about Children

The above discussion centred around the production of those programmes which are "for children". It would be equally important to discuss the production of programmes which are "about children"and meant for adults—parents, teachers and other adults. It would be important at the outset to indicate that if the production of programmes for children is meagre, programmes about children are almost negligible. Hence, it is difficult to discuss them in each of the three categories outlined in the framework in Chapter I.

At present, on every Saturday a programme is telecast for primary school teachers in all the INSAT areas. These programmes are produced by CIET. Basically, these programmes are supposed to be viewed by the teachers to improve their teaching ability. At present, there are no studies available to indicate the effectiveness of such programmes or the extent to which these programmes are actually viewed by the teachers. Details about the production methods of these programmes are not immediately available, though class-room lecture format seems to be a well-accepted method and sometimes documentary formats are also used. Central Institute of Educational Technology has taken the lead in the production of these programmes, having academic resources at their disposal to produce such programmes.

Recently UNICEF has introduced short duration 'spots' which are directly addressed to adults (especially parents), to get them to protect their children from several childhood disabilities through preventive means. These programmes have been produced by outside agencies with the help of UNICEF experts. The actual method of the production of these programmes is not fully known, but it is clear that these are high-cost programmes in which a large amount of inputs have been provided by the content experts.

At this point, special mention must be made about a monthly programme known as *Palavi*. This is produced at Bombay Doordarshan Kendra by a woman producer having a post-graduate degree in arts and in education, and with basic television programme production training at Pune. Her idea needs to be commented upon, for, this idea gave her a chance to get into the depths of a child's heart and mind. In addition to her regular production of children's programmes, she has taken the unenviable task of producing this monthly Marathi programme. It is mainly for parents, both urban and rural, of all classes on the theme of bringing up children. In order to produce this programme, extensive format research was conducted by the producer herself to know the problems children face in school vis-a-vis teachers, parents, neighbours and others. The producer went around twenty-five schools, including an *adivasi* one, covering all strata of society. She asked about 5000 children to write on a piece of paper what troubled them most and assured them that their paper would not be shown to their teachers or other school authorities. She had a fantastic response. Out of these problems she then selected, purely subjectively, about twenty-five of the biggest problems children faced. Some of these were—

— Teacher talks about hazards of bad habits while chewing pan.
— At home, parents scold me; at school, teachers use harsh words; in the neighbourhood, people abuse me. I wish some people would

tell me what is good in me.

— At home my father beats my mother regularly, and here at school they ask us to respect elders.

Finally the gem of a thought.

"Why only intelligent students are taught well and pampered, when we at the bottom of the class, who require maximum attention stand neglected."

The producer arranged a panel discussion with representatives of parents, teachers and sociologists. Students as interviewers expressed the opinions gathered, entailing comments and explanations of adults. In the producer's own words, "the response was so overwhelming that like a Nobel prize winner, I rested on my laurels for quite a while."

The same producer, produced another programme on SSC-passed students, who had obtained 80 per cent marks and above, but were living in *Zopadpattis* (hutments) or on pavements. When she interviewed the students and showed visually the home environment of the students who had obtained high marks, many people called up and gave help in both cash and kind to the economically-deprived achievers.

CIET Production

Special mention is also required about CIET's production process, since CIET is directly responsible for the production of enrichment programmes for children. As indicated in Chapter 1, the CIET production process differs from Doordarshan's. The following paragraphs analyse and bring out their method of production.

At present, there are seven production teams with four inhouse script writers, an adequate number of researchers and good, up-to-date production facilities. The quantity of production here is the same as that of Upgrah Doordarshan Kendra, New Delhi. However, even with such numbers and facilities, CIET is not able to make the total of about 200 programmes per year required to keep the telecast going. It was mentioned that, in their view, it is not necessary to produce 200 programmes as they feel that even with a lesser number, the telecast schedule can be met by repeating good-quality programmes. Therefore, quality is of prime importance, and CIET claims to be very quality conscious. Not that they are fully satisfied with their current quality; but they are striving hard to achieve the highest quality.

The CIET programmes are intended for enrichment school telecast as well as for out-of-school rural children. CIET reasons that since the drop-out rate in schools in the rural areas is very high, it does not make sense to address programmes to only in-school children. Their programmes are meant to be enrichment programmes, with special emphasis on activities which the children can do on their own after viewing the programmes. Every year a national workshop is convened in which the topics are decided, objectives written, and series planned. Based on these, a book of briefs is written to facilitate the work of the producers. Scripts are written by the in-house script-writers in the majority of cases, but outside script writers are also commissioned for this purpose. In fact, CIET has a very pragmatic approach and would be utilising outside production teams as well to produce programmes. The scripts go through a script committee before they are finalised, and are modified if necessary. Similarly, programmes are previewed by an in-house committee comprising largely of professional staff and the inputs are incorporated in future productions. Apart from being activity oriented, the programmes should foster a desirable attitude in children. This was very clearly expressed by the Director, though no explicit statement to that effect was made by any member of the production staff.

As far as research is concerned, CIET has made a good beginning, it has gone into almost all aspects of programme development as well as utilization and follow-up. CIET also has the responsibility of the management of morning telecast. In respect of the formative research, they have carried out work on needs assessment in a few States, compiled audience profiles on video and pretested few sample scripts. However, they are still a long way from concluding what will make their programmes more effective for the target audience. The intentions are good and they are working in the right direction. It will of course, take a much greater effort to systematise what they have started. At present, the following lacunae have been observed:

1. No attempts have been made to conduct a comprehensive full-cycle formative research on any of the programmes. That is to say, right from the stage of writing the objectives in a measurable form to operationalizing it, discussing it with the content specialist, writing the script, examining it for information load, logical sequence, getting it modified, pretesting it, modifying it, rehearsing and producing it, telecasting it and studying its impact.
2. The team mode of production has not caught on. The Director spoke of the production team, but his 'team' means the technical

staff and does not include the researcher or the script writer.

3. The producers on the whole have no rural orientation or feel and thus like the Upgrah Doordarshan Kendra, New Delhi, producers are at a loss to know whom they are programming for. Unless these lacunae are removed, no worthwhile programmes can be produced. A video profile is a little better than a descriptive profile, but it cannot replace what a producer can see in the field himself/herself.

CIET has an advantage of having the facilities to train and arrange training courses, and it should use these to remove any gaps in the knowledge and skills of its production staff.

ISRO Production

Beginning with SITE, ISRO has been involved in the production of children's television programmes. This and other related activities are now the responsibility of ISRO'S Development and Educational Communication Unit. It has been producing children's television programmes, following the team-mode of production initiated by ISRO during SITE for the production of science education programmes. Children's programmes are produced by producers who are also involved in the production of other development programmes. After SITE, programme production by ISRO has continued as part of the Kheda Communications Project (KCP), all productions are based on a 'CREDO', which provides the basic guidelines for all the programme production and the communication strategy for education and development. It follows a series of production steps that are broadly discussed in Chapter 4. Basically, seven steps have been followed in the production of Children's Television Programme after having done the need assessment and preparing a profile of the children of Kheda district (See Joshi, 1978).

The steps are :

1. Discussion about the ideas for children's programmes with educational authorities and other members of the production staff.
2. Formative research inputs for production, constitution of the production team and development of scripts.
3. Script committee discussion for the approval of the script (the committee consists of producers, script writers, communication researchers and other production staff).

4. Programme production, followed by a preview and discussion.
5. Programme pretesting: Some of the programmes are pretested before a series of programmes are produced on the given topic. Also, pretesting is done to decide on format, content, information load and other aesthetic aspects of the programme.
6. Feedback on about ten per cent of the programmes is also collected, for improvement and modification of future programmes.
7. Analysis of viewers' letters, some of which are responded to on television.

ISRO, though being in the operational mode, differs quite a bit from Doordarshan production methods. ISRO takes into consideration the diverse needs of different age groups and their aspirations and beliefs. The production team regularly visits the villages where their target audience live, and gets frequent feedback from the audience.

Other Organisations

In the context of the real need for children's programmes, the efforts of both CIET and ISRO are but drops in the ocean. Both have commitment, resources, trained human power and comparatively more time at their disposal to produce such programmes. Probably it is for this reason that their productions reflect better quality, both in terms of presentation techniques and content. Considering the linguistic and cultural diversity, plurality of religions and economic disparities one would require many production centres like these if children's television has to make some impact in our country.

There are several other institutions within the country which can help produce programmes for children. For example, the Indian Council of Medical Research has accumulated much knowledge about the health needs of children in rural and urban slum areas in many parts of the country. However, there has been no attempt on their part to produce any kind of television programmes on health to educate the children. Nevertheless, it is important to note that the Council can play a role in evolving such programmes by collaborating with production centres.

The Centre for the Development of Instructional Technology (CENDIT), New Delhi is well-known for its efforts in developmental programmes. It has worked in rural areas, with various objectives and target groups. They have not ventured in the field of children's television programmes, though are gearing up towards it and are in the planning and experimental stage. CENDIT does seem to have the potential for making meaningful programmes for children. They have done a good deal of serious thinking, trying to find out how children can be served more responsibly and responsively as far as evolving television programmes for them are concerned.

The National Institute of Public Cooperation and Child Development (NIPCED), New Delhi, plays an important role in training the staff of the national health and human services delivery project known as Integrated Child Development Services (ICDS). But it has made little effort to develop anything worth the name as "material for children", leave aside television programmes. However, in recent times, it has become aware of this need, and is intending to move systematically to do something to correct it. The institute would first like to document what is available and then plan for the development of its own material. However, this is the opinion of a concerned professional at the institute and not necessarily the official viewpoint of the Institute. Again, since this institute possesses a great deal of knowledge on children, their health and nutrition needs and problems, and allround development, it can play a part in collaborating with other organisations to produce television programmes for and about children.

Child Media Lab (CML) has existed at the NCERT, New Delhi for almost a decade now. This place is a storehouse of knowledge on children's development. Their efforts till now have been mostly in evolving children's literature, educational toys and games. They have also made radio programmes for children, but have not ventured into the arena of television production. They do have plans to do so, but have no expertise whatsoever on television. They could be trained in television production, or can collaborate with other organisations to produce television programmes for children. It is not out of place to mention that they have very little interaction with CIET, which is also a part of NCERT. Efforts should be made to bring them together for this purpose.

Two other institutions where children's programmes could be produced are:

(i) Central Institute of Indian Languages (CIIL), Mysore, and
(ii) Central Institute of English and Foreign Languages (CIEFL), Hyderabad. Both these institutions have produced language-teaching programmes for children. At present, they are experimenting with video for the production of language-teaching

programme. While CIEFL has moved into the production of programmes for higher education (i.e. university-level), it is still a very good place for producing programmes for teaching English and other foreign languages to children. CIIL too could produce programmes for language teaching in the country.

Chitrabani in Calcutta, and St. Xaviers' Institute of Communications, Bombay are other places that could also be considered for the production of children's programmes. Also, there are several individual producers sensitive to children's issues who could also be asked to take the lead in programme production.

Programme Philosophy

It is essential that there be a programme philosophy or Credo for children's television, whether "for children" or "about children", enrichment or syllabus-based. Such a Credo is necessary, because it would give direction and coherence to the programmes and serve as a guideline to organizations and individual producers. One of the ideas promoted here, keeping in view the cultural and linguistic diversities, relates to the concept of "pro-social" and educational television.

We think that children's television ought to be 'pro-social' that is, making programmes which are designed to influence the young viewer in a positive way. This involves a value judgment and usually refers to both psychological and behavioural influences. On the psychological level, prosocial television should enhance the child's feeling of self-worth, confidence and ability to deal with an everincreasing complex world; and, on the behavioural level, it should enhance the child's repertoire of actions and skills which permit effective interaction with others and his/her environment. There are several criteria to judge the prosocial television:

1. Does the television experience expand how the child learns? Does it give him or her the cognitive skills, the curiosity and the behaviours through which the child seeks greater knowledge and understanding so that she/he can continue to mature as an individual and as a member of the society?
2. Does the television experience expand her/his knowledge?
3. Does the television experience expand his/her repertoire of behavioural and social skills necessary in dealing with other children and adults?

4. Does the television experience expand the child's repertoire of emotional experience and skills? Can she/he learn to be more spontaneous in her/his displays of friendliness and humour?
5. Can it help the child think, evaluate, feel and have verbal and cognitive skills?

If television fosters these, it is worth the name of prosocial television. One quick and easy way of determining the appropriateness or prosocial nature of the programme is by getting an answer to a few questions given below:

1. Does the programme appeal to the child?
2. Does the programme present different groups positively and does it show them in situations that enhance the self-image of a child whether she/he be rural, urban, tribal, rich, poor, servant or master?
3. Does the programme present gender roles and adult roles positively?
4. Does the programme present social issues that are appropriate for the child viewer and perhaps are something a child can act on at a child's level?
5. Does the programme encourage worthwhile ideals, values and beliefs?
6. Does the programme present conflict that a child can understand and does it demonstrate positive strategies for reducing the conflict?
7. Does the programme stimulate constructive activities and does it enhance the quality of the child's play?
8. Does the programme separate fact from fantasy? Does it separate advertisements from programme content?
9. Does the programme present humour of a child's level? Or is it adult ridicule or an adult remembering what he thought was funny from his/her childhood?
10. Does the programme have a pace that allows the child to absorb and contemplate the material presented?
11. Does the programme have artistic qualities?

These are only some of the questions that are raised here. But more questions could be evolved for this purpose.

The production of pro-social television programmes requires a production process that follows a sequence ultimately leading to an effective programme. Such a programme cannot and should not be left to an individual's imagination and creativity. Several aspects of the production process need to be carefully planned by a team of experts from several specialities leading to what is popularly known as the "team mode of production", which has been referred to on several occasions earlier. A short description of the team mode of production follows:

TEAM MODE OF PRODUCTION

Television programmes for children need coordination and team effort among several kinds of professionals like Script writers, Cameramen, Researchers, Content experts, Child psychologists and Producers. For children's television programme production, further complexity is added due to the involvement of "content-matter expert and educationists who are looking for a measurable gain-in-knowledge of the children. As indicated earlier, varying degrees of team-mode of production have been attempted at various centres of production. During SITE, ISRO produced science education programmes in a team mode. The success of these programmes, and the experience of continuing this mode in Kheda and in a few other centres, has brought out the need and utility of the team mode, especially for children's television programmes. Almost every producer interviewed expressed the feeling that the production process should be a team effort, in which every member of the team should be committed to meaningful and relevant programmes. In this mode, each member of the team shares the production responsibility at every stage of production. Typically, a team consists of a producer, script writer, subject-matter expert, communication researcher and other members of the production crew. The team works together from the inception to the realization of the programme. Keeping the team mode of production in view, specialized training for all the production staff has been suggested. Aghi, Agrawal and Ramanathan (in Press) observed that "with the time factor playing such a crucial role, most of the producers mentioned that if every crew member was a specialist in his area, be it a lighting assistant or a floor manager, it would help in communicating one's requirements and instructions better and getting the job done faster and much more efficiently". Their observation further strengthens the view that training of the entire production crew is a necessary condition for producing a good educational television programme.

Production Equipment

Ten years after SITE, one observes much less equipment constraints for children's programme production. Both funds and equipments are available. However, it is equally true that these facilities are not well-distributed, with some stations having excellent facilities and others being poorly equipped. As indicated in Chapter 1, more than one-fourth of the children's programmes are in black & white even now, and in some places like Cuttack, almost all the children programmes are being telecast in black & white (see Table 1.4 in Chapter 1). Also, specialised equipments for the production of children's programmes are not available in most places. However, it is noted that equipment in general does not pose a serious hindrance for specialized production. Outdoor equipment too is made available provided proper advance planning is done, though one observes quite a bit of *ad hocism* in such production planning. It has been also observed that outdoor equipments, studio facilities and personnel are drawn from a central pool in each station, and there are no dedicated facilities for production of children's programmes.

Programme Formats

Gill (1984) suggested three major formats namely "use of life characters", 'puppets' and 'animation' for producing children's programmes. Advantages and limitations of other formats have been discussed by Gill and Luthra (in Press). At present, selection of format is based on several considerations other than educational and learning, like time allotted for the production etc., as indicated earlier.

In most parts, for literature/language, history, environment and science programmes, play formats or dance-cum-music, dance ballets, singing are resorted to as it requires fewer visuals and little or no efforts for locating or recording such material. While producing science programmes, the cameras are directly taken to the school or college laboratories, or simulated laboratories are created in the studio and explanations are provided 'on camera'. In almost all cases decisions regarding format selection are made on the basis of the producer's instincts and experience and viability of programme production at a breakneck speed. Use of puppets is resorted to once in a while.

Little experimentation, whether in content and format, has been observed, and rarely have several formats been utilized in sequence. Due to existing rules for hiring talent (including comperes) not more than once a month, it is very difficult to build a "talent-team" for better production. On the other hand, in ISRO and CIET, since detailed briefs with objectives, content, and "questions to ponder over" are designed with the full involvement of the production team, even formats of such programmes get evolved in the process. For example, during the production of "exclusive school programmes" by ISRO, a drama format got evolved in which a "question answer session" formed the last part of the programme. Script testing, and programme pretesting both help in determining the suitability of a format, and this is discussed in Chapter 4.

Training

Analysis presented so far indicates the need for trained human power for the production of children's television. It is clear that though there is training available for general production personnel, little efforts have been made to train specialized producers for children. Though persons having education degree and experience with children are generally selected as "children's programme producer" initially, they move out from this work and are assigned to other 'important' productions. Gill (1984:259) points out that "selection of producers is at best haphazard. Children's programmes are considered child's play —producers who are under-utilized at the television centre—and sometimes even those who are incompetent at their work—are allocated to the children's programme section...[Specialized] training after selection is either non-existent or, once again haphazard. Similarly placement of trained personnel are made arbitrarily". In the light of Gill's observations and other observations made during this study, training of producers of children's programmes is essential. It is suggested that a separate in-service training of 150 working days should be arranged for creating a cadre of children's television producers. Initial selection of producers and production assistants should be from among those having background in education, child development and psychology. This training should be carefully designed in consultation with media trainers, educationists and communication researchers. Some of the broad areas of training are given here.

Survey of Children's Television

Educational and development potential, limitations of the medium; introduction to mass media showing their relationships to social, cultural, political, educational and economic process within the broad national framework.

Television and Learning

Effects of television programmes on learning by children.

Team Mode of Production

Task and role of various team members and programme personnel (Producer, Production Assistant and others), communication researchers, content expert, educator and others. Discussion on some of the earlier televised children television programming—its success and failure. Effects of programme on forming children's tastes and opinion.

Television Production Techniques

Should include production and direction, camera techniques, sound and editing techniques, genre of programmes, content and format selection, visualization and use of special effects. Understanding of various steps of research and their utility in the production process. Perfecting specializing in specific production-direction skill—with special emphasis on children's television, instructional design. Understanding and hands-on experience for the production of cultural programmes, such as drama, music and dances. Special problems, and unique advantages of roving camera techniques, use of graphics, animation, puppets and other forms. Actual hands-on experience in all the steps of team mode of production is indicated in Chapter 4.

3

TECHNOLOGY FOR CHILDREN'S PROGRAMME PRODUCTION

THERE are clear indications that though equipment is available for the production of children's television, it is either not adequate or not easily available to the producers. Some analyses have been presented in the previous Chapters. In this Chapter, efforts have been made to provide emerging trends in Video technology and its effects on the production methods and techniques. It will be followed by a short discussion on the special equipment required for the production of children programmes and training needs.

Emerging Trends in Video Technology

The technological advances in recent years have been so great that a system unthinkable few years back is a reality today. Its impact is being felt in every domain of human endeavour. Video technology is no exception. These advances have facilitated the incorporation of more number of functions, reliable operation, ruggedization, precision, automation and ease of operation. This was only possible with the use of Very Large Scale Integrated (VLSI) circuit technology, universal use of digital techniques coupled with the great progress in the area of computer technology.

The VLSI technology: integrated circuits in simple form were a novelty a decade ago. Then, certain functions were added to generate the Large Scale Integrated Circuit. These days, a number of functional blocks are integrated to create an identifiable sub-system block. This has reduced the circuitry to such a level that the most complicated processes and functions are possible with manageable hardware. This has led to miniaturization and has enhanced the speed of operation.

The second revolutionary trend has been the use of digital techniques. Digital techniques, with their distinct advantages over analog counterparts, have won the final battle. Now every conceivable television studio operation is being converted into a digital one. A complete digital studio today is a real entity. Every studio process and equipment (from camera output till the signal is carried out of the studio) is digital. Recording, pre/post processing and editing functions are done in a digital environment. The images captured via the camera pick-up tubes can be preserved without any noise perturbations till their final exit from the studio.

The third and most powerful event has been the entry of computers and microprocessors into the video field. This process was accelerated through the extensive use of VLSI and digital technology. Generation of graphics, drawing and painting of still pictures, generation of special effects, two-dimensional real-time animation, three-dimensional image synthesis and animation are some of the best demonstrable current applications of computer-aided systems. More realistic and high quality three dimension (3-D) images can be generated by using a model which is made up of mathematical surfaces. The computer calculates algorithms, according to given conditions of position, size and rotation of model and generates 3-D images. It is now possible to have a real time frame-by-frame animation system. The artist can build objects, establish animation key frames and run animation sequences. It is possible to have high definition 3-D objects moving in a real three dimensional world. Move the object, move the viewer, move the light source and travel with objects, see it with reality. Graphics are an integral part of animation and 3-D objects generation system. Computer graphics systems these days combine the functions of a Character Generator, graphic or system, 2D and 3-D animation into one image system. The possibilities seem endless.

Besides these major areas the advances in Charge-Coupled Devices (CCD) and laser technologies have also contributed tremendously to the video field. Stereoscopic solid state CCD TV camera systems are available now which have high sensitivity, improved resolution, high linearity, geometric fidelity and spectral range superior to vidicon tube camera system. Laser beam recording has created an exciting possibility of applying this technique to design a high density broadcast-quality video recorder. Laser beam recording also provides high brightness, sharp directivity and good monochromaticity. Some of the technologies will soon be getting integrated into the Indian Television production system, both within Doordarshan and outside Doordarshan. Special care is required to select those technologies needed especially for children's television programme production.

Technology Gap

The studio equipment which exist in Doordarshan, CIET and other organisations is mostly meant for general programme production. The same is being used for children's programme with very little specific children's programme production facilities. Large part of children's programme are on education in instructional or in discussion formats which require only general facilities. Large part of equipment being used for this purpose is capable of producing programmes in black and white as the studies/discussion reveal that the old studio facilities are being used for making children's programmes.

In fact, it is probably children's programmes more than any others, that really need to be produced in colour to be effective. Besides, the latest techniques equipment being used these days makes the use of colour equipment absolutely necessary because of compatibility requirements. The general facilities existing at the moment at most of the places also require augmentation in terms of special children's programme production facilities. In the present circumstances, it would be desirable to set up two levels of studios in addition to what is already existing for the purposes of research, training and proto-type production which is very important given the cultural and linguistic complexity in the country. The studio equipment suggested in Table 3.1 could be used in the proposed Centre for Children's Television or Children's Television Laboratory (for details, see Chapter 5). The second kind of studio referred to as low cost studio is suggested for use by "independent" production organisations (i.e. other than the traditional media organisations). The details of the equipment for such studio is given in Table 3.2. However, special equipment for children's production being complex and expensive, could be available centrally at the Centre for Children's Television or Children's Television Laboratory, indicated in Table 3.3.

Technical Training

Programmes for children basically require a lot of work on animation, graphics and special effects generation. The equipment for these functions provides extensive facilities and creative choices to such an extent that imagination to exploit their capabilities seems to be the only limitation. A very close man-machine interaction can bring out the best from the equipment and translate the imaginative ideas into reality.

This is only possible if the personnel handling such equipment are trained in their specific areas of specialization. Besides, the equipment used for recording and editing is becoming so sophisticated that only proper training can produce the best results. The areas in which the training is specifically essential for children's programme are the following :

Graphics/Paint Box	8 man months
Special effects	6 man months
Animation	4 man months
Editing/Post-production operations	12 man months
	30 man months

TABLE 3.1 : **List of Studio Equipment, Technical Manpower and Space for the Proposed Centre along with Low Cost Equipment**

			*Rs. (in lakhs)**	
S. No.	*Equipment*	*Qty.*	*Broadcast quality*	*Low Cost*
Video Equipment				
1.	Studio TV Camera	3	48.00	30.00
2.	1" VTR	3	165.00	—
3.	3/4" Highband VTR	3	24.00	—
4.	3/4" Lowband VTR	4	—	8.00
5.	TV Camera (outdoor)	2	7.00	1.00
6.	3/4" VTR (Portable outdoor)	2	4.00	1.80
7.	9" Monitor	8	2.80	0.80
8.	14" Monitor	8	3.20	1.60
9.	20" Monitor	2	1.20	0.80
10.	26" Monitor	1	0.75	0.40
11.	Waveform Monitor	1	2.10	0.70
12.	Vectroscope	3	2.25	0.90
13.	16 input switcher with 3 level mixer	1	26.00	10.00
14.	Digital Special effect	1	30.00	10.00
15.	Video Processor	1	2.00	2.00
16.	Sync. Generator & Changeover unit	2	1.00	0.25
17.	VDA (one in 10 out and 8 modules)	3	0.78	0.78
18.	PDA (one in 10 out and 8 modules)	2	0.50	0.50
19.	Telecine	1	60.00	10.00
20.	DTBC	1	2.00	2.00
21.	Animation Equipment	1	10.00	3.50
22.	Video Graphics with Character Generator	1	5.00	1.50
23.	Paint box	1	13.00	2.00
24.	Colour encoder	1	0.30	0.30

(Contd.)

TABLE 3.1 — *Contd.*

S. No.	*Equipment*	*Qty.*	*Rs. (in lakhs)** *Broadcast quality*	*Low Cost*
25.	Test Signal Generator	1	1.00	1.00
26.	Test Pattern Generator	1	0.50	0.50
27.	Video Editing Equipment (3/4")	1	0.50	0.25
28.	Battery Charger	4	0.20	0.20
29.	Miscellaneous Items		5.00	2.00
			418.08	92.78
Audio Equipment				
1.	Microphones	10	0.50	0.50
2.	12 Channel Audio Mixer	1	6.00	1.00
3.	Tape Recorder	2	3.00	3.00
4.	Distribution Amplifier (one in ten out and 8 modules)	2	0.40	0.40
5.	Audio Generator	1	0.20	0.20
6.	Miscellaneous Items		1.00	0.50
			11.10	5.60
Maintenance Equipment				
1.	Oscilloscope	1	1.00	1.00
2.	Tool Kit (set)	2	0.20	0.20
3.	Multimeter	2	0.04	0.04
4.	Camera Maintenance and Test Kit	1	3.00	—
5.	VTR Maintenance Kit	1	3.00	—
6.	Waveform Monitor	1	1.00	1.00
7.	Logic Analyser	1	3.00	3.00
8.	Vectroscope	1	1.00	1.00
9.	Frequency Counter	1	1.00	1.00
			13.24	7.24
	Grand Total		442.12	105.62

Technical Manpower (one shift operations)	
Engineer-in-charge	1
Office-typist	1
Engineer SC/SB	1
Technical Asstts. B/C	2
Tradesman (Recording/editing/CCU/Switcher/Telecine/Operations)	6
Helper	1
Total	12

(*Contd.*)

TABLE 3.1 — *Contd.*

Equipment	*Quantity*	
Space		
A. Air Conditioned Space	*Sq. Mtrs.*	
Studio	100	
Control room	30	
VTR/Editing room	50	
Instruments Lab	20	
Dimmer room	10	
Tape Library	20	
	230	
B. Non Air-Conditioned Space		
Stores	20	
Airconditioning Plant/Electrical installations and maintenance	60	
	80	
C. Sitting Space for Technical Manpower		
Engineer-in-Charge	20	
Office	10	
Engineer	10	
Technical Asstts.	10	
Tradesman	20	
	70	
Cost Estimate	*(Rs. in lakhs)*	
Capital Cost	*Broadcast quality*	*Low Cost*
Studio Equipment	442.12	105.62
Installation and Commissioning	30.00	20.00
Total	472.12	125.62
Yearly operations and maintenance cost for studio and test equipment	Rs. 45.00 lakh	Rs. 10.00 lakh

*Excludes customs duty.

TABLE 3.2 : **List of Low Cost Studio Equipment**

*(Rs. in lakhs)**

S. No.	*Equipment*	*Qnty.*	*Cost*
Low Cost Studio			
1.	3 Tube Camera with CCU	3	15.00
2.	Highband 3/4" MTR	3	6.00
3.	Switcher, Mixer, effect	1	5.00
4.	Telecine (without camera)	1	2.00
5.	Sync. Generator with Changeover unit	1	1.00
6.	Video Processor	1	2.00

(*Contd.*)

TABLE 3.2 — *Contd.*

*(Rs. in lakhs)**

S. No.	*Equipment*	*Qnty.*	*Cost*
7.	Monitor 14"	10	3.00
8.	Monitor 20"	3	1.20
9.	Waveform Monitor	2	0.40
10.	Vectroscope	2	0.50
11.	VDA	3	0.80
12.	PDA	2	0.50
13.	TBC	2	1.00
14.	Editing Equipment	1	0.30
15.	Battery Charger	2	0.10
16.	Video Patch Panel	1	0.10
17.	Outdoor Camera	2	1.00
18.	Portable VTR	2	1.20
19.	Camera Stand	3	2.40
20.	Camera Lens	5	0.65
21.	Audio Mixer	1	1.00
22.	ADA	2	0.40
23.	Audio Pitch Panel	1	0.05
24.	Audio Tape Recorder	2	1.00
25.	Audio Amplifier	1	0.04
26.	Microphones (Condensor/Dynamic)	8	0.90
27.	Speaker System	1	0.05
	Total		47.59

*Excludes customs duty.

TABLE 3.3: **List of Special Studio Equipment for Children's Programme**

*Cost (Rs. in lakhs)**

S. No.	*Equipment*	*Broadcast quality*	*Low Cost*
Augmentation of existing Studio facilities for Children's Programme			
1.	Animation	10.00	3.50
2.	Video Graphics with Character Generator	5.00	1.50
3.	Paint Box	13.00	2.00
4.	Digital Special Effect	30.00	10.00
		58.00	17.00

*Excludes customs duty.

4

RESEARCH FOR CHILDREN'S TELEVISION

AT PRESENT, television research within Doordarshan is divided between rural and urban viewers. While "Audience Research Units" are focusing their attention on the evaluation of programme preferences and programme rating of individual television-owning urban viewers, the Research and Evaluation cells are involved in the formative researches related primarily to rural viewers of community television. Most of Doordarshan's audience researches are centrally designed and planned from its headquarters located in Delhi, as a part of the Directorate General of Doordarshan.

As indicated in Chapter 1, several formative researches have been conducted by Doordarshan staff in the INSAT states. But now that the production responsibility of children's educational programmes lies with CIET and SIET, gradually such researches seem to be of less importance to Doordarshan research staff, and much of its research excludes children viewers. Actually, CIET and the SIET's are today producing only about 50% of the children's programmes, and a substantial proportion of the production continues to be done by various Doordarshan Stations.

So far, most of the researchers of Doordarshan have followed a 'sender-oriented' approach (Rao, *et al.,* 1982). In this Chapter, an effort has been made to suggest 'receiver-oriented' research. This, of course, will call for significant organisational and management changes both in style and content. These issues will be discussed in detail.

At this point, it is equally important to dispel the myth that research for children's programme production is costly and time-consuming. Experiences within the country and outside country have shown that investment in research is cost-effective. Also, once a proper system is set up, it does not delay the production process. In fact, it facilitates and smoothens programme production. It is in this perspective that the research recommendations have been made. Television research for effective children's programmes is fairly recent anywhere in the world. The best known example is Children's TV Workshop (CTW), where communication researchers have demonstrated their worth in producing most effective programmes for children using what is now known as the "CTW Model", a unique blend of planning, production and research (Palmer 1983). Its objective was to employ entertaining television to provide pre-school children with useful learning experiences.

"The CTW model is based on the sequence of plânning and research steps followed in the creation of Sesame Street to achieve an effective three-way collaboration among researchers, producers and outside advisors" (Young, 1983:12). "The CTW model is unique in educational planning. It ensures that goals are carefully set, that the talent and expertise of researchers, producers, and academics are pooled, and that the risks of failure are minimized by the attention that is paid to formative research" (Young, 1983:15).

Formative Research in Television Production in India

Formative research in television production has, in one way or another, been employed since 1960, when the first educational television programmes were produced in India. But the first formal reference to formative research appeared during SITE, from one of the psychologists trained in Children's Television Workshop, and a few others with background in social sciences or media research. The "SITE model" which was initiated in 1974, continues to be utilized in various television production organisations in one form or other. Essentially the CTW model provided a useful reference point" (Trivedi, in Press). The SITE model was quite general, and was used for the production of "instructional programmes" in various age categories and on variety of developmental topics. Specific use of the SITE model for science education programme production is most appropriate for the present discussion, along with its use for another serial meant for rural children of Kheda. (See Aghi, in Press and Trivedi, in Press). Doordarshan and other educational television production institutions like Central Institute of Indian Languages (Mysore), Central Institute of Educational Technology (New Delhi) and Film & Television Institute of India (Pune), have basically emulated the SITE model for the production of children's television. To elaborate the SITE model, it would be best to outline the sequence of planning and research steps followed in the production of SITE science education programmes for children of 5 to 12 years age, studying in the primary schools (class I to V) in rural areas.

The planning sequence and research steps can be summarized as follows:

1. Assessing needs and characteristics of the children television viewers.
2. Defining Educational/Instructional objectives.
3. Developing Educational and Communication Strategies and Writers Briefs.
4. Script Writing and Testing.
5. Pre-testing Programmes.
6. Process Research.
7. Summative Research.

In addition to these steps, observations indicated that the definition and role of research, learning in a team mode of production, development of interpersonal skills to work in a team and creation of a management system conducive to this approach are also important.

All the steps in one form or other must be followed in order to produce relevant and effective programmes of high quality. Each of these steps are elaborated in the following paragraphs.

ASSESSING NEEDS AND CHARACTERISTICS OF CHILDREN TELEVISION VIEWERS

In the Indian sub-continent it would be most difficult to define who is an average child. Even at the regional level, this question cannot be answered without qualifications. Hence, several methods can be followed to overcome this problem of identifying the child's needs for whom the programmes are to be produced. One of the simplest method suggested is that a 'Workshop' of educators, educational planners, child psychologists, producers, and script writers along with parents, school teachers and communication researchers should be called in a given geographical linguistic region to discuss the needs of the children. It will also help in deciding the future line of action and in formulating ideas. Another argument is that such Workshops really do not contribute in formulating or sharpening the ideas. Instead, it unnecessarily reinforces the existing beliefs of the experts in the absence of any fresh field-based data to begin with. In the States where research-based data is available, the Workshop approach will be more useful, whereas in the States where there is a lack of basic data, initial field research would be most desirable. These two options should be kept in view while initiating researches related to the children's need assessment studies.

Workshop

The purpose of the Workshop is to bring together professionals with specialized knowledge and experience and those who will get directly affected by the television programmes—that is children, parents and teachers. The Workshop should be planned and organized by the agency responsible for overall education and developmental planning and coordination of the programme production and transmission. The Workshop should be of two to three days duration and should also be attended by government officials working in the various educational and development departments, health, nutrition and child development. Special efforts should be made to have experts who could address some of the questions that should be raised in the workshop like:

1. What can television do for children in general and out-of children in particular?
2. What needs are capable of being met through television exposure in community and home television viewing?
3. What are the socio-psychological areas in which television can provide viable solutions to the children?
4. What are linguistic, cultural and economic impediments to children's learning from television?
5. How can television—independently, and in conjunction with other media—facilitate learning of children in a given linguistic region?

Based on the recommendations of the Workshop, detailed field-based investigations must be conducted to assess the children's need.

Assessing Needs of Children

All the needs of the children should be assessed within the cultural and linguistic context, keeping both sexes in view. Some of the questions that must be raised include issues like: What are children's activities at home, and in community, at school and play, both of boys and girls together and separately?

What are the problems and difficulties they encounter in the same context? What would they like to become as grown-up adults; their needs, ambitions and creative interests? How do they interact with their elders (parents, teachers and other elder members of the village and caste), and other children; what kind of notion do they have about caste hierarchy, differences between men and women, rich and poor; what are their belief systems and what are their educational and information needs?

The study must be very qualitative and in-depth, and should be conducted at regional level. It should be conducted with care and preplanning and with the cooperation of educationists and child development experts. All efforts should be made to draw analyse sharply focused qualitative insights and not just figures.

These needs assessment studies must contribute in providing data to help plan means and ways by which television intervention can help in enhancing scientific understanding on the child's part. This kind of research should be conducted by taking a cross- sectional sample at the regional level. Also, some data should be collected at micro-level to provide an in-depth understanding.

Profile of the Children

An in-depth descriptive profile of the children must be developed as an input to the programme producers by the communication researchers. The profile must provide detailed data on the linguistic behaviour of the children. As indicated in Chapter 1, language seems to be a central element in deciding the success/failure of the programme. Hence, linguistic analysis will be very important. Efforts should also be made to develop 'visual profiles' by way of still photographs and video presentation approach of both 'typical' and 'atypical' children of a given linguistic region. To provide factual data, a holistic approach should be followed. The profile should be descriptive, along with detailed statistical data about children of the region. Existing educational and other developmental plans for the children and about children must be integrated in the profile. Special mention must be made about the social environment of the children in various age categories. This must be analysed separately for both sexes as there will be perceptible differences in the total environment of the boys and girls. The assistance of child psychologists might help in determining some of these differences and its implications for programme production.

Based on needs assessment and profile of the children within the socio-cultural milieu, an attempt should be made to analyse the problem and define the needs amenable to television intervention. An illustration would further help explaining the value of these researches. After conducting a need assessment study among the rural children, Trivedi (in Press) reported, "based on our discussion on the observational data and picture of the child and the village situation, we attempted to analyse the problem and define the needs. The situation suggests that the feelings of dependency and powerlessness reduces one's action ability and motivation to act upon the environment— this further leads to experience of lack of control over environment and again generates the feelings of helplessness, frustration and resignation . . . . the need was to break the vicious circle by developing positive attitude and skills in the child and increasing his resourcefulness and his motivation for achievement and action which in turn will lead to successful outcome and a feeling of confidence in effecting changes in his environment".

Defining Education/Instructional Objectives

The third important research step is to define the objectives of the programmes based on the identification of the children's needs. The objective must be divided into "broad goals" and "specific programme goals". These goals must be defined in consultation with the production team and programme briefs should be prepared to enable the script writer to prepare scripts for script testing. It would be equally important at this point to discuss resources, and whether the objectives can be met within the production time limits if specified. This would further help in narrowing down the goal. This process needs to be repeated to reach a meaningful and well-defined objective of a programme or series of programmes.

The starting point for this exercise has to be the overall objective. This can then be sub-divided into objectives for each series or group of programmes. Within each of these, every individual programme too must have a defined goal or objective. The aim is to begin from the known (what the child already knows) and lead him/her through a series of learning experiences to what is presumably unknown to him/her. Thus, each programme builds on the last, creating a cumulative effect and moving step by step towards the defined overall objective.

Communication Strategies

In developing the communication strategy, it is necessary to consider and define the support that other media can provide, and to plan for this. Co-ordination of such multi-media efforts, is obviously extremely difficult, especially if one is dealing with widely dispersed target audience or in rural areas. However, the additional advantage of such support from other media makes the effort worthwhile. The planning of the TV programme would have to take into account the availability (or non-availability) of such support, so that the programme is either part of a total package or has "stand-alone" capability.

Another important element of communication strategy is the type of programmes— whether they are one-shot programmes or part of a serial. In the latter case, one can have episodic serials in which each part is self-continued, or non-episodic ones, where there is continuity of story-line from one part to the next. In situations of uncertain audience continuity (due to set breakdown, lack of electricity, holidays, etc.), the former is obviously preferable.

Regardless of the topic, keeping in view the cultural context while conceiving a programme or series of programmes, it is essential to provide a broad guideline for suggesting possible formats to communicate the educational message in the programmes. The suggestion should emerge from the existing literature, past experiences and research studies. For example, if the programme is being produced for community television in the 'evening general telecast', emphasis on visual rather than verbal presentation should be considered most desirable. The consideration here is that both educational and communication strategies must be kept in view to concretize the educational objectives.

Writer's Briefs

Given the cultural diversity and the lack of first-hand knowledge of rural and poor children on the part of most script writers, it is essential to elaborate the educational objectives. As far as possible, illustrations should be provided to the script writer keeping the target children in view and the communication strategy. For example, if the target group belongs to a rural area, visit to the rural areas will help to identify rural situations and conditions, method of responding and reacting to the problems. These observations then can be incorporated in the writers brief. It is also suggested (as is already being followed to some extent by CIET) to prepare a script writer's manual that "would include a strategy, a take off point, appropriate situations and the behavioural outcome for each objective" (Trivedi, in Press).

Script Testing

Time and again, experience in India strongly suggest that even before proceeding on a trial production, it is essential that script testing be done in the field situation. Aghi (in Press) based on her SITE experiences observed "of all the steps that are to be followed by a formative researcher, script testing emerged to be something which was extremely crucial". Script testing provides a quick and cheaper method (than programme pretesting) for assessing needs and the level of the children's knowledge for a particular concept. Generally, a joint session of the production team helps in suggesting approach, plot, characters and situations to the script writer, who— in turn — drafts the script keeping in view the specific objective of the programme. This draft script goes through a discussion phase among the producer, subject matter specialist and communication researcher to ascertain whether the narration emphasizes strongly and effectively, without any contradiction and ambiguity, the basic message. Also, whether the plots and dialogues (if any) are appropriate in the light of the characteristics of the television viewing children and the script is production worthy (see Trivedi, in Press). After making appropriate modifications, a script is taken to a selected group of actual television viewers for script testing which involves reading of the script to a selected group of children in a story telling manner and questioning them about the meaning of all the difficult words and concepts. The script should also be tested for overall comprehension and its interest-holding ability. The responses of the children are noted and are discussed with subject matter specialists, script writer and producer. Basically, the whole team gets involved in the process. Modifications in the language and message are done by the script writer. Sometimes, a script is written in different formats and these scripts are tested to choose one which is considered to be the most effective. Script testing in the cultural context of each linguistic sub-region is very essential because of dialectical and "social class" differences, even within a single linguistic region. The efforts should be to use those spoken words which are comprehensible to the largest majority of the children. "The process then continues, carrying it to story boards, picture boards and to the combination of visual and audio before the decision is reached for final production" (Aghi, in Press).

Programme Pretesting

Communication researchers play a crucial role in pretesting of the "pilot programmes". At the initial stages, while developing a new serial, different versions of the same programme can be produced and pretested for its comprehension and recall. Even when this is not possible, pretesting of one of the programmes, using the proposed format and approach, can provide valuable feedback to modify future programmes. Some of the key issues involved in the pretest are given below for general use.

1. What kind of language will be understood by the children of a given linguistic region?
2. What kind of visuals will be understood and will hold the attention of the children?
3. What format would be interesting and aid in the child's comprehension of new ideas?
4. How much content should be put into a given programme of what duration?
5. How should the content be placed sequentially within the programme?
6. What features enhance the credibility of the presenter/compere?
7. What kind of presenter/compere would be most effective in children's programme?
8. What kind of presentation would be most effective for children's programmes?
9. What kind of characters and settings would have the most credibility for children of various socio-cultural backgrounds?
10. To what extent is there an internal compatibility —consistency in conveying the theme without any inherent contradiction?
11. What was the level of appeal, attractiveness and attention- holding power of the programme?
12. Was the "pace" of the programme appropriate?

Typically, a qualitative indepth approach should be followed for programme pretesting. It involves showing the programme to a selected group of children representing the target audience. Observation of the children during the preview session, in-depth interviews of the individual children and also group discussions are all necessary. A flexible approach should be employed to suit the field situation. In other parts of the world, children are brought to studio or specially designed media laboratory for pretesting. But in the Indian context, the pretesting has to be done in the field situation since the target audience is often far from television production facilities. Trivedi (in Press) provides the actual steps that need to be followed.

It is important to note that pre-testing findings are necessarily specific to the particular combination of message-script-format-approach, and as such there is danger in trying to overly generalize them.

Process Evaluation

Process evaluation or feedback studies provide the immediate reaction of the children, teachers and parents. Given that television is one-way communication, feedback is the second best way to have "live" contact with the audience —children both in school and outside the school. Feedback would provide detailed insights on, among other things, how children responded to the programme in terms of interest, comprehension, credibility and utility. Process evaluation data is also utilized in the production of future programmes. A panel can be formed for regular feedback. Also, occasional feedback studies should be conducted to know the viewing situation, viewing problems, and other factors affecting television viewing.

Summative Research

Media organisations, decision-makers, production teams, and educationists raise a basic question: What was the effect of the programmes in terms of achieving the defined objectives? In order to answer such a question, summative research is conducted to measure the impact or effect of the programmes. Such research requires a full understanding of the programmes, their content, objectives, defined target audiences and expected educational gains. A variety of research approaches are available to conduct summative research. Both qualitative and quantitative researches should be conducted. In order to measure precise impact, field experimental design should be employed. Further, it is preferable that such researches be conducted by outside research agencies—i.e., an agency not directly involved with the production of the programmes. For formative and process research, an internal team must be a part of the production team and should be trained in the team mode of production.

TRAINING FOR COMMUNICATION RESEARCH

It must be clearly recognized that none of the institutions within India are training communication researchers for the purposes defined in this Chapter. It is, therefore, essential to provide in-service training for communication research by selecting from amongst the social scientists especially those with a background in child psychology, child development, social anthropology, sociology and education.

The four main areas in which training would be most essential are:

1. To work in a production team as one of the members of the team, and understanding the production process;
2. To have an excellent grasp of communication theories and processes and educational technology;
3. Re-orientation in research methods with special emphasis on formative research for television production; and
4. Training to assist in appropriate design of television messages for children and their utilization by the children both in community television and home viewing situations.

Special training should be designed for this purpose. There are two approaches to conduct their especially designed training: "production team" approach and "specialized" training approach. No matter which of the two approaches is followed, about ten weeks of training will be required to cover the theoretical and practical aspects. In addition, at least two productions must be done in the team mode of production. To begin with, this training can be given by bringing together a group of specialists who will evolve course material from both international and national experiences. This course material should then be reproduced for future use, with detailed guidelines for its wider use. As the need for such training would increase over a period of time, the training material should have broader scope of use and flexible courses should be designed.

5

TRAINING AND MANAGEMENT

IN THE previous three Chapters, training and human power requirements in production, engineering and research have been reflected. In this Chapter, these will be integrated to outline the training approach and requirements along with recommendations for places of training, production management and structure.

It is amply clear from the earlier discussions that children's television programme production requires a team mode of production. The basic philosophy of training should centre around this concept, as it is difficult to achieve if not fostered from the beginning.

TRAINING FOR TEAM MODE OF PRODUCTION

As indicated on several occasions and particularly in Chapters 2 and 3, team mode of production for children's television programmes is essential. Such an approach helps to reduce uncertainty, improves the quality of programme and ensures its positive effects. Past experiences within India provide ample evidence to show that this approach is practical and especially useful where programmes are to be produced in multiple languages. It is also a "felt need" of the producers and media production organizations. Typically, a production team consists of producer, communication researcher, subject matter/content expert, script writer and other members of the production team. Instead of an individual, the team takes the responsibility of the production, from its inception to final realization of the programme. Training for such a team would differ from the general television production training presently imparted to in-service Doordarshan staff at Film and Television Institute of India, Pune, and Development and Educational Communication Unit, ISRO, Ahmedabad. Short term collaborative courses conducted at Central Institute of Educational Technology (CIET) partially caters to this kind of need. Hence, it is suggested that a detailed training programme should be worked out. This training programme should be a specialized one in which except subject-matter/content specialist and every other member of the team should go through regular training. An attempt has been made to evolve one such training syllabus for the 'production team' of educational television. This syllabus can be modified and improved upon after field testing its usefulness and also the duration can be modified, depending upon the needs. However, it is also equally important to train the subject-matter specialist to understand the limitations and potential of the medium and to interact with the production team. This could be done through a short term training course of three to four weeks duration. Keeping in view the recent advances in video technology, further efforts should be made to develop special training courses for both production and engineering staff as suggested in Chapter 3. Details of such specialized training should be worked out, keeping in view the needs and goals of children's programmes.

GENERALIZED *VS.* SPECIALIZED TRAINING

There is a recurrent discussion about generalized and specialized training. In this context, there is some discussion whether 'enrichment', 'exclusive' and 'general' telecast programmes 'for' and 'about' children belong to a different genre of production techniques, requiring training of a different kind. However, it is argued here that the basic philosophy and requirements of general training outlines are adequate for these different purposes and do not need any changes. At the same time, specialized training to each category of production personnel like communication researcher, script writer, producer and other production staff is equally important. It is suggested that specialized training should be considered as a sequential activity to be given only after general training. However, special training to the engineering staff at the time of acquiring new equipment must be arranged separately. At present, almost all training courses in the country are confined to those who are already in a regular job, giving rise to special emphasis on 'in-service' training. There are several advantages of such a training approach. At the same time, it does not permit others to get a chance to do independent production. Keeping this in view, efforts should be made to train individuals to create a 'bank' of independent production teams, outside the traditional media organisation. It will also help in developing healthy professional competition, and thereby improving the quality of production.

Training Needs

Based on the existing needs of Doordarshan for children's television producers, it may seem a futile exercise to think of separate training for production staff. However, if one keeps in view the INSAT television telecast needs and the recommendations of the Working Group on Software for Doordarshan (which has recommended 15 to 20 per cent of total telecast time for children), then the number of such production teams needed will be very large. Even if we do not increase the staffing pattern of Doordarshan, CIET and SIETs, about one-fifth of the total production team should have special training in the production of children's television. Keeping these aspects in view, there will be a need for training of more than 100 production teams to begin with, requiring an equal number of all kinds of specialists. Existing professional training courses have the capacity to cater to only a small number of production crew. Therefore, training will have to also provide for strengthening the basic learning in production techniques. It is for this reason that the syllabus includes these areas. It is recommended that persons having post-graduate degrees in social science, especially psychology, child development and education, should be inducted after appropriate selection for their aptitude to work with children and in a team. The existing educational system will provide these kinds for persons.

Based on the estimation of human-power requirements, and the existing facilities, two strategies are suggested for meeting the training requirements:

1. Existing in-service training centres should be requested to devote one training course out of three for children's television.
2. Effort should be made to create a Centre for Children's Television or a Children's Television Laboratory at the national level, fully dedicated and well-equipped to take full responsibility of the training, research and prototype production of programmes. The detailed requirements of hardware and engineering staff are given in Chapter 3. The software human-power requirements would depend upon the production responsibility that this centre takes on. In addition, training staff on the pattern that exists in FTII, with special augmentation of communication researchers, would suffice to meet the present requirement. However, the type of

professional required would be different and should be carefully selected. This centre should act as a place of excellence for children's television. Given the requirement of training, it would remain busy for the next five years catering to the needs of the traditional media organisations.

BIBLIOGRAPHY

Aghi, Mira (1977) What TV can do in Children's Development Programmes? Paper presented at the International Congress of Paediatrics, New Delhi.

Aghi, Mira (In Press) "The Role of Research in the Production for Science Education Programmes for SITE Children—A Case Study", *In Television and the Indian Child —A Handbook.* (eds.) Binod C. Agrawal and Mira Aghi. New Delhi: UNICEF.

Aghi, Mira; Binod C. Agrawal and A. Ramanathan (In Press) "Producers Perspective on Children's Programmes", In *Television and the Indian Child: A Handbook* (eds.) Binod C. Agrawal and Mira Aghi. New Delhi: UNICEF.

Agrawal, Binod C. (In Press) Television Expansion and the Indian Child: A Historical Perspective. In *Television and the Indian Child: A Handbook* (eds.) Binod C. Agrawal amd Mira Aghi. New Delhi: UNICEF.

Agrawal, Binod C. and Mira Aghi (eds.) (In Press) *Television and the Indian Child : A Handbook.* New Delhi : UNICEF.

Agrawal, S.C. and S.V.S. Choudhary (1984 a) Rural Children and Television Programmes. New Delhi: Upgrah Doordarshan Kendra.

Agrawal, S.C. and S.V.S. Choudhary (1984 b) Need Assessment Study of Educational TV Programmes—Rural Areas of Jaipur. New Delhi: Upgrah Doordarshan Kendra.

An Indian Personality for Television (1985) Report of the Working Group on Software Plan for Doordarshan, New Delhi: Ministry of Information and Broadcasting, Government of India.

Annual Report 1983-84 (1984) Ministry of Information and Broadcasting, Annual Report 1983-84. New Delhi: The Directorate of Publications Divisions, Ministry of Information and Broadcasting, Government of India.

Behari, S. and Gopal Gupta (1979) Content Inputs for Formal Education

Series on Television. New Delhi: Upgrah Doordarshan Kendra.

Bhaskaran, P. assisted by I. Patel (1977) SITE for Children: Morning Feedback. Ahmedabad: Space Applications Centre.

Gill, Rina (1984) Television for Children. *Vidura,* Vol. 21, No. 5, pp. 255-261.

Gill, Rina, and Sunanda Luthra (In Press) Educational Television: Developing Programmes for Children. In *Television and the Indian Child: A Handbook.* (eds.) Binod C. Agrawal and Mira Aghi, New Delhi: UNICEF.

Goel, R., (1984) *Educational Television in India: Organisation and Utilisation.* Post Doctoral Thesis submitted to M.S. University of Baroda, Baroda.

Joshi, S.R., (1978) Mode of Operation, Seminar-232 - Another TV. pp. 36-40.

Kumar, Narendra and K. Jayramchandi (1967) *Educational Television in India,* New Delhi: Arya Book Depot.

National Guidelines for Educational Broadcasting (1983) National Guidelines for Educational Broadcasting. New Delhi: Ministry of Education and Culture, Government of India.

Neurath, Paul, *School Television in Delhi.* New Delhi: All India Radio.

Palmer, Edward L. (1983) The CTW Model in U.S. Children's Television Workshop International Research Notes. 4, pp. 4-6.

Phutela, R.L. (1984) *A Study into Utilisation and Comprehensibility of School Television Programmes in Delhi.* New Delhi: Central Institute of Educational Technology, NCERT.

Rahman, S., (1977) Educational Television (Udayabhanu), Satellite Instructional Television Experiment. An Exploratory Study of Educational Satellite Broadcast Television Programme in Orissa, New Delhi: Ministry of Education and Social Welfare.

Rao, T.V., M.S. Sayadain and S. Sreenivas Rao (1982) *Audience Research Units of All India Radio and Doordarshan,* Ahmedabad: Indian Institute of Management.

Report of Working Group on Educational Technology (1978) Report of Working Group on Educational Technology. New Delhi: Ministry of Educational and Social Welfare, Government of India.

Sehgal, Narender K. (ed.), (1979) *Technology Transfer in Communications: Television Broadcasting in India.* Ahmedabad: Space Applications Centre.

Shukla S, and K. Kumar (1977) *SITE Impact Study on Primary School Children.* New Delhi: NCERT.

Singh, J. and Singh A.K., (1984) *A Study to Assess the Needs of the Primary School Children of Orissa for Educational TV Support,* New Delhi : Central Institute of Educational Technology, NCERT.

Television in India 1985 (1985) Television in India 1985. New Delhi : Audience Research Unit, Directorate General, Doordarshan.

Trivedi, Neela (1977) *Aiming at Motivation for Improvisation: An Experiment in TV for Rural Children.* Ahmedabad: Space Applications Centre.

Trivedi, Neela (1977) Feedback Report of *Dada No Dongoro Leedho.* Ahmedabad: Space Applications Centre.

Trivedi, Neela (In Press) Realisation of Psycho-Social Objectives: An Experiment in Television for Rural Children. In *Television and the Indian Child - A Handbook* (eds.) Binod C. Agrawal and Mira Aghi, New Delhi: UNICEF.

Young, Susan A., (1983) The CTW Model. Children's Television Workshop, International Research Notes. Issue No. 4, pp. 12-15.

INDEX